California Bucket List Adventure Guide

*Explore 100 Offbeat
Destinations You Must Visit!*

Cynthia Bennett

Canyon Press
canyon@purplelink.org

Please consider writing a review!
Just visit: purplelink.org/review

ISBN: 978-1-957590-03-5

FREE BONUS

Discover 31 Incredible Places You Can
Visit Next! Just Go To:

purplelink.org/travel

Table of Contents

How to Use This Book

Welcome to your very own adventure guide to exploring the many wonders of the state of California. Not only does this book offer the most wonderful places to visit and sights to see in the vast state, but it provides GPS coordinates for Google Maps to make exploring that much easier.

Adventure Guide
Sorted by region, this guide offers over 100 amazing wonders found in California for you to see and explore. They can be visited in any order, and this book will help you keep track of where you've been and where to look forward to going next. Each section describes the area or place, what to look for, how to get there, and what you may need to bring along.

GPS Coordinates
As you can imagine, not all of the locations in this book have a physical address. Fortunately, some of our listed wonders are either located within a National Park or Reserve or near a city, town, or place of business. For those that are not associated with a specific location, it is easiest to map it using GPS coordinates.

Luckily, Google has a system of codes that converts the coordinates into pin-drop locations that Google Maps can interpret and navigate.

Each adventure in this guide includes GPS coordinates along with a physical address whenever it is available.

It is important that you are prepared for poor cell signals. It is recommended that you route your location and ensure that the directions are accessible offline. Depending on your device and the distance of some locations, you may need to travel with a backup battery source.

About California

The gorgeous state of California has been drawing people from near and far for centuries. The Golden State earned its official nickname from the Gold Rush in 1848, which attracted over 300,000 people to the territory. On September 9th, 1850, California became the 31st state to join the United States of America, soon becoming the most populous U.S. state.

Stretching for nearly 900 miles, California is the third-largest state by land area in the U.S., bordering Mexico to the south. Altogether, California boasts a total land area of 163,694 miles. Although highly populated throughout, most of California's residents live near one of its four large cities: Los Angeles, San Diego, San Jose, and San Francisco.

Landscape and Climate

California offers a stunning variety of terrains and climates due to its extensive size, including cliff-lined beaches, mountains, valleys, deserts, and forests. It is home to some of the most exceptional trees in the world, millions of acres of farmland, and an abundance of natural beauty. In fact, the highest and lowest points of the contiguous 48 states are both located in California.

The diversity of California doesn't stop at its landscapes. The great expanses of wilderness and several national parks provide habitats for thousands of species of plants and animals.

Generally, California's climate varies by area, depending on latitude and proximity to the ocean. A majority of California's climate is considered Mediterranean, with warm, dry summers and mild, wet winters. Cities on the coast experience maritime climate, while inland locations like Central Valley can be quite hot in the summer. Frigid climates are found in the higher mountainous areas, while desert regions are prominent in the area known as Death Valley.

Amboy Crater

Amboy Crater is an extinct cinder cone volcano that overlooks a lava field. It is estimated to be around 79,000 years old and is found in the eastern Mojave Desert. In 1973, the crater was designated as the Amboy Crater National Natural Landmark. For a superb view of the surrounding landscapes, you can hike to the top of the crater. The trail will take you 944 feet above sea level, 250 feet above the surrounding land, and is accessible using the Western Cone Trail.

Best Time to Visit: The best times to visit Amboy Crater are during winter or early spring.

Pass/Permit/Fees: There is no fee to visit Amboy Crater.

Closest City or Town: Amboy, California

Physical Address:
Roy's Motel and Café
87520 National Trails Highway
Amboy, CA 92304

GPS Coordinates: 34.5439° N, 115.7911° W

Did You Know? The volcano last erupted 10,000 years ago, transforming the surrounding landscape.

Disneyland

Disneyland California is the only amusement park that was designed and completed under the direct supervision of Walt Disney. It opened in the summer of 1955 and was the first Disney theme park. This magical theme park offers different areas such as Fantasyland, Tomorrowland, and New Orleans Square with immersive rides and attractions. Disneyland hosts more than 18 million people each year and has entertained over 726 million people since opening.

Best Time to Visit: Disneyland is open Monday through Thursday from 9:00 a.m. to 9:00 p.m., Friday from 9:00 a.m. to 11:00 p.m., Saturday from 8:00 a.m. to 12:00 a.m., and Sunday from 8:00 a.m. to 11:00 p.m.

Pass/Permit/Fees: Ticket prices to visit Disneyland vary but start at $76 per day, per person.

Closest City or Town: Anaheim, California

Physical Address:
1313 Disneyland Drive
Anaheim, CA 92802

GPS Coordinates: 33.8129° N, 117.9190° W

Did You Know? There are nine "lands" in Disneyland: Adventureland, Frontierland, Fantasyland, Tomorrowland, Main Street, U.S.A., New Orleans Square, Critter Country, Star Wars: Galaxy's Edge, and Mickey's Toontown.

Lava Tube - Mojave Desert

This particular lava tube in the Mojave Desert is the subject of many photographs. It is famous for the small holes in the ceiling that allow a cascade of light to filter into the dark cave. The small dust particles in the air appear to dance in the beams of light while providing a tranquil backdrop to the subterranean cave. The cave is about 500 feet long, 3 feet tall at its shortest, and about 10 feet wide in other places. The hike to the entrance is only about a quarter of a mile and takes you over tar-black volcanic rocks on a small incline. There is a metal ladder descending into the tube. Please remember to bring a flashlight!

Best Time to Visit: The best time to visit the Lava Tube in the Mojave Desert is midday in the spring when the sun is overhead.

Pass/Permit/Fees: There is no fee to visit the lava tube.

Closest City or Town: Baker, California

Physical Address:
Mojave National Preserve
2701 Barstow Road
Barstow, CA 92311

GPS Coordinates: 35.2163° N, 115.7515° W

Did You Know? This lava tube formed approximately 7.6 million years ago.

Bass Lake

Bass Lake is a reservoir that was created in Madera County to supply the first hydroelectricity in the state of California. The lake is five miles long and is billed as a smaller version of Lake Tahoe. However, at a lower elevation of 3,400 feet, Bass Lake is much more pleasant to visit in the summer. Sailing, water-skiing, wakeboarding, wave running, kayaking, and pedal boating are all popular water activities at Bass Lake. As its name suggests, it is also a favorite fishing location, with bass, rainbow trout, Kokanee salmon, and other fish species readily available in the waters.

Best Time to Visit: The best time to visit Bass Lake is in the summer.

Pass/Permit/Fees: There is no fee to visit Bass Lake.

Closest City or Town: Bass Lake, California

Physical Address:
Yosemite Bass Lake Welcome Center
54354 Road 432
Bass Lake, CA 93604

GPS Coordinates: 37.3213° N, 119.5720° W

Did You Know? Between October and April, visitors to Bass Lake may encounter mono winds, a localized strong wind phenomenon that features gusts over 80 miles per hour.

McWay Falls

Highway 1 along the Bur Sur Coast is described as the "longest and most scenic stretch of undeveloped coastline in the contiguous U.S." Along the way is an overlook trail that features a stunning waterfall known as McWay Falls. This 80-foot waterfall drops onto a lovely beach cove. Visitors are prohibited on the beach area, so the cove remains natural. The water flows all year round and, during high tide, it can fall directly into the ocean. There are two ways to access the McWay Falls Overlook Trail, a 0.6 mile round trip trail to view the falls. You can either park along Hwy. 1 for free, or you can access the trail while visiting the Julia Pfeiffer Burns State Park.

Best Time to Visit: The best times to visit McWay Falls are during spring or early summer for the wildflowers.

Pass/Permit/Fees: There is a $10 entry fee to Julia Pfeiffer Burns State Park to visit McWay Falls.

Closest City or Town: Big Sur, California

Physical Address:
52801 CA-1
Big Sur, CA 93920

GPS Coordinates: 36.1578° N, 121.6722° W

Did You Know? McWay Falls is one of two tide falls in California, along with Alamere Falls.

Pfeiffer Beach

You'll want to visit this hidden gem while near the Big Sur Coastline. It's even better to visit Pfeiffer Beach at sunset when you have the best photo op of The Keyhole Arch, where you can see waves crashing through the natural arch. However, there are other dramatic rock formations besides Keyhole Arch at Pfeiffer Beach. At the north end of the beach, there is unique purple sand from the manganese garnet rocks in the cliffs. Swimming is not advised due to potentially dangerous currents, and the water is cold. A bit off the beaten path, Pfeiffer Beach is well worth the drive, though there is no signage posted or visibility from the highway. Camping and fires are not allowed.

Best Time to Visit: For a picturesque sunset, visit Pfeiffer Beach between mid-December and mid-January.

Pass/Permit/Fees: There is a $12 fee per vehicle and a $12 parking fee.

Closest City or Town: Big Sur, California

Physical Address:
9100 Sycamore Canyon Road
Big Sur, CA 93920

GPS Coordinates: 36.2381° N, 121.8162° W

Did You Know? The extreme north side of the beach is on federal land and is sometimes clothing optional.

Ancient Bristlecone Pine Forest

Located in the Inyo National Forest, the Ancient Bristlecone Pine Forest is home to bristlecone pine trees, the oldest trees in the world. Many of these trees are over 4,000 years old! Stop in at the Schulman Grove visitor center to get information about the trees, then head to the Patriarch Grove, where you'll find the largest bristlecone pine tree in the world. Known as the Patriarch Tree, its isolation and remoteness make for an extremely striking photograph. The ages of these trees have caused them to grow in twisted knots, which means they'll all be different and beautiful in their own right.

Best Time to Visit: The best time to visit the is during the summer, as the road closes with winter snowfall.

Pass/Permit/Fees: There is a $15 fee per person to visit.

Closest City or Town: Bishop, California

Physical Address:
351 Pacu Lane
Bishop, CA 93514

GPS Coordinates: 37.3861° N, 118.1784° W

Did You Know? The Patriarch Tree is believed to be 5,070 years old, which means it was approximately 500 years old when the Giza pyramids were built and 3,000 years old when the English language was developed.

Bishop Creek

Located in Inyo National Forest in eastern Sierra Nevada, Bishop Creek is a 10.1-mile stream that has three forks, which all flow into lakes: North Lake, Sabrina Lake, and South Lake. There is also a reservoir called Intake Two along the way, and Bishop Creek meets Owens River past the city of Bishop. There are several incredible views in this area, including the canyon, surrounding mountains, and alpine forests. Camping, fishing, bouldering, and motorboating are popular activities, along with scenic hiking. For convenient access, there is parking near each of the lakes.

Best Time to Visit: The best time to visit Bishop Creek is in the fall.

Pass/Permit/Fees: There is a $5 fee per person to visit Bishop Creek.

Closest City or Town: Bishop, California

Physical Address:
Inyo National Forest
351 Pacu Lane
Bishop, CA 93514

GPS Coordinates: 37.26583° N, 118.57806° W

Did You Know? Bishop Creek is at an elevation of about 7,400 feet.

The Slot Canyon

Located in Anza Borrego State Park, this natural formation is part of a 2.3-mile loop trail. The "Slot" is located about two miles down a dirt road, but it's easy to miss, so keep a look out! It's also suggested to check in with the visitor's center before heading to the canyon. Once you find it, you may want to mark your entrance with rocks to guide you back to your exit. As you proceed into the "Slot," the canyon grows taller and narrower. Along the way is a natural rock bridge across the top, and after the bridge, the canyon opens up to a dirt road.

Best Time to Visit: The best time to visit the Slot Canyon is between September and May.

Pass/Permit/Fees: There is a $10 fee to visit the Slot Canyon.

Closest City or Town: Borrego Springs, California

Physical Address:
Anza Borrego State Park
200 Palm Canyon Drive
Borrego Springs, CA 92004

GPS Coordinates: 33.1820° N, 116.2141° W

Did You Know? The canyon was formed by flash floods, and at some points the walls reach 40 feet high. The canyon floor gets as narrow as 1 foot.

Big Basin Redwoods State Park

Established in 1902, Big Basin Redwoods State Park is the oldest state park in California. It is located in the heart of the Santa Cruz Mountains and features ancient coast redwood trees, many of which are over 50 feet in diameter and as tall as the Statue of Liberty. These trees are between 1,000 and 1,800 years old and are thought to predate the Roman Empire. Big Basin Redwoods State Park contains the largest continuous stand of redwood trees south of San Francisco, featuring both old-growth and recovering second-growth redwood forest areas. Additionally, there are more than 80 miles of trails throughout the park.

Best Time to Visit: This park is ideal for visiting during any time of the year.

Pass/Permit/Fees: There is a $10 fee per vehicle.

Closest City or Town: Boulder Creek, California

Physical Address:
21600 Big Basin Way
Boulder Creek, CA 95006

GPS Coordinates: 37.1676° N, 122.2512° W

Did You Know? The redwood trees in Big Basin can live to be over 2,500 years old.

Knott's Berry Farm

Knott's Berry Farm began as a small roadside berry stand in the 1920s and eventually grew into the world-famous theme park it is today. It was originally founded by Walter Knott, whose family began selling fried chicken dinners and tea on his property in 1934. By the 1940s, his enterprise had a restaurant called Mrs. Knott's Chicken Dinner Restaurant, along with various attractions. In the 1950s, the idea of operating an amusement park took root, and Knott opened what he called a "summer-long county fair." The park continued to grow, and in 1968, he began charging admission to the grounds.

Best Time to Visit: Visit Knott's Berry Farm is in June, preferably during the week, to avoid weekend crowds.

Pass/Permit/Fees: General admission for visitors ages three and up is $99 at the gate.

Closest City or Town: Buena Park, California

Physical Address:
8039 Beach Boulevard
Buena Park, CA 90620

GPS Coordinates: 33.8445° N, 118.0002° W

Did You Know? Annual special events at Knott's Berry Farm include Knott's Scary Farm during October and Knott's Merry Farm in December.

Petrified Forest

Approximately 3.4 million years ago, Mount St. Helena erupted and began the creation of the Petrified Forest in Sonoma County, California. The largest preserved trees in the world are found in the Petrified Forest. These giant redwood trees, which laid beneath volcanic ash for millions of years, have fossilized. The trails here offer the unique experience of journeying through the only preserved ancient forest from the Pliocene Epoch. There are trails that provide views of Mt. St. Helena, the extinct volcano whose powerful eruption knocked down the prehistoric forest of Redwoods. The Petrified Forest Walk is only 0.9 miles. There are guided tours every Wednesday through Sunday and self-guided tours all day long during open hours.

Best Time to Visit: Visit the forest during spring and fall.

Pass/Permit/Fees: There is a $10 fee per vehicle to visit the Petrified Forest.

Closest City or Town: Calistoga, California

Physical Address:
4100 Petrified Forest Road
Calistoga, CA 94515

GPS Coordinates: 35.0037° N, 109.7889° W

Did You Know? The same family, the Bockees, have operated and maintained the forest for more than 100 years.

Carlsbad Ranch

For six to eight weeks every spring, Carlsbad Ranch features 50 acres of Giant Tecolote Ranunculus flowers. These are known as the "Flower Fields at Carlsbad Ranch." From early March through early May, the fields burst with color and announce the arrival of spring. The fields have been cultivated for more than 85 years and were first planted in the early 1920s by settler Luther Gage. The flowers were so successful that Gage was able to operate a flourishing business called "Luther Gage Giant Tecolote Ranunculus Bulbs."

Best Time to Visit: The best time to visit Carlsbad Ranch is during April to see the blooms.

Pass/Permit/Fees: Admission is $22 per adult, $10 per child aged three through 10, and $20 per senior-aged, 60 and over, and military members.

Closest City or Town: Carlsbad, California

Physical Address:
5704 Paseo Del Norte
Carlsbad, CA 92008

GPS Coordinates: 33.1512° N, 117.3101° W

Did You Know? Luther Gage named the flowers that bloom in the Flower Fields at Carlsbad Ranch "Tecolote," after the owls that nested on his property.

Point Lobos

Often referred to as "the crown jewel of the State Park Systems," Point Lobos State Natural Reserve attracts over one million people each year. Great for sightseeing, photography, nature study, scuba diving, jogging, and painting. Rare plant communities, unique geological formations, endangered archaeological sites, as well as land and sea flora and fauna are all found in the area. As one of the richest marine habitats in California, the Point Lobos State Marine Preserve can only be explored by certified divers, and reservations are requested. If you have an hour to spend, take the Cypress Grove Trail for excellent rocky shoreline views.

Best Time to Visit: The best times to visit Point Lobos are fall or spring.

Pass/Permit/Fees: There is a $10 fee per day, and diving fees to reach Point Lobos vary.

Closest City or Town: Carmel-by-the-Sea, California

Physical Address:
Carmel-by-the-Sea Visitor Center
Ocean Avenue
Carmel-By-The-Sea, CA 93923

GPS Coordinates: 36.5159° N, 121.9382° W

Did You Know? The name is derived from the offshore rocks at Punta de Los Lobos Marinos.

Lake Almanor

Lake Almanor is a reservoir located in Plumas County that was formed by the Canyon Dam on the Feather River, Benner Creek, Last Chance Creek, Hamilton Branch, and several natural springs. The lake was created in 1914 as part of a project to create hydroelectric power, but in the process, it displaced several Yamani Maidu Native American families who were living in the valley. Today, the lake still generates hydroelectricity, but it is also a popular recreation area, providing many opportunities for fishing, boating, swimming, water-skiing, and more.

Best Time to Visit: Visit during spring and summer.

Pass/Permit/Fees: There is no fee to visit Lake Almanor.

Closest City or Town: Chester, California

Physical Address:
Lake Almanor Area Chamber of Commerce
278 Main Street, Suite 3
Chester, CA 96020

GPS Coordinates: 40.2724° N, 121.1836° W

Did You Know? Lake Almanor is named for the three daughters of Great Western Power's Vice President Guy C. Earl. The first two letters of Alice and Martha and the last two letters of Eleanor were combined to create Almanor.

Cima Dome

Famous for its impressive dome shape, Cima Dome is a massive 70-acre dome that covers 70 square miles. Its lack of foliage creates a smoothness that looks like the lens of a camera, and its nearly perfect symmetry rises 1,500 feet above the surrounding Mojave Desert. Teutonia Peak Trail winds through the densest Joshua Tree Forest in the world and to the top of a rocky, 5,755-foot mountain on the edge of Cima Dome. There are also silver mines covered by grates along the way. You can view this unusual geological feature from a distance by looking northwest from Cedar Canyon Road, 2.5 miles east of Kelso Cima Road.

Best Time to Visit: The best time to visit Cima Dome is between March and April for carpets of wildflowers

Pass/Permit/Fees: There is no fee to visit Cima Dome.

Closest City or Town: Cima, California

Physical Address:
Kelso Depot Visitor Center
90942 Kelso Cima Road
Kelso, CA 92309

GPS Coordinates: 35.2894° N, 115.5853° W

Did You Know? Cima Volcanic Field is west of Cima Dome and consists of around 40 volcanic cones and nearly 60 lava flows.

Marshall Gold Discovery State Historic Park

In 1948, the discovery of gold changed California's history forever. John Sutter's discovery of gold nuggets at his sawmill site in Coloma triggered a mass migration to the West Coast, an event that is known as the 1949 Gold Rush. At Marshall Gold Discovery State Park, you can learn about the discovery of gold, hike the gold rush-era trails, and even pan for gold yourself. The Gold Discovery Tour tells the story of the Coloma Valley both before and after gold was found there.

Best Time to Visit: The best time to visit is during the spring or fall when the weather is milder.

Pass/Permit/Fees: There is a $10 fee per vehicle to visit the park and a $3 fee per adult ($2 per child) to take the Gold Discovery Tour.

Closest City or Town: Coloma, California

Physical Address:
310 Back Street
Coloma, CA 95613

GPS Coordinates: 38.8011° N, 120.8923° W

Did You Know? The San Francisco 49ers are named after the year the Gold Rush began in California.

Dana Point Harbor

Dana Point Harbor is often referred to as the "Dolphin and Whale Capital of the World" because it is one of the top locations for whale-watching. Depending on the time of year you go, you'll see gray whales in the winter and blue whales in the summer. Dana Point Harbor also boasts various recreational amenities, such as boating, surfing, dining, and shopping. Visitors are treated to spectacular sunsets and stunning views while they shop, dine, or play. The harbor is also home to the Festival of Whales, the Tall Ships Festival, and the Holiday Boat Parade, among other events that occur annually or on a one-off basis.

Best Time to Visit: The best time to visit Dana Point Harbor is during the winter for gray whale-watching and the spring and summer for blue whale-watching.

Pass/Permit/Fees: There is no fee to visit.

Closest City or Town: Dana Point, California

Physical Address:
The Marina at Dana Point
34571 Golden Lantern Street
Dana Point, CA 72629

GPS Coordinates: 33.4635° N, 117.6958 W

Did You Know? Swimming is open at the family-friendly Dana Point Harbor Beach, also known as "Baby Beach."

Artist's Palette

A unique venture to take in Death Valley National Park is known as Artist's Drive. This scenic route takes you through canyons and past mountains that are covered in various colors. The main stop at the end is Artist's Palette, which features colorful rocks and soil. The oxidation of metals and elements from the ground produces these vibrant hues. The entire route is a 9-mile, one-way loop. There is a parking lot along the way, so you can also access the viewpoint on foot.

Best Time to Visit: The best time to visit Artist's Palette in Death Valley is between November and April.

Pass/Permit/Fees: To enter Death Valley National Park, there is a $30 fee per vehicle, a $25 fee per motorcycle, or $15 fee for visitors on foot, bike, or horse.

Closest City or Town: Death Valley, California

Physical Address:
Death Valley National Park Post Office
328 Greenland Boulevard
Death Valley, CA 92328

GPS Coordinates: 42.5306° N, 75.5235° W

Did You Know? The colorful oxidation of the minerals is evidence of the area's explosive, volcanic periods.

Badwater

Death Valley National Park is full of mountains, salt formations, sand dunes, and an enormous crater. One of the most popular driving routes is known as Badwater Road. Badwater Basin — the lowest point of land in the western hemisphere — is 282 feet below sea level and hot all year round. Surrounded by mountains, Badwater Lake is shallow and rimmed with salt. The conditions and time of year affect the water level, and when there's no water, you can walk onto the basin's thick layer of salt on the valley floor. There's also a boardwalk across the basin.

Best Time to Visit: The best times to visit Badwater in Death Valley are in winter or late fall.

Pass/Permit/Fees: There is a $25 fee per vehicle that is valid for seven days.

Closest City or Town: Death Valley, California

Physical Address:
Death Valley National Park Post Office
328 Greenland Boulevard
Death Valley, CA 92328

GPS Coordinates: 36.2461° N, 116.8185° W

Did You Know? Badwater Basin is home to a species of minute salt marsh snail called the Badwater Snail.

Death Valley National Park

The largest national park in the contiguous United States and the hottest and driest of any park in the country, Death Valley National Park encompasses land in both California and Nevada. It also occupies the area between the Great Basin and Mojave deserts. Visitors to the park will find that it is home to the second-lowest point in the Western Hemisphere, the Badwater Basin, and the tallest mountain in the contiguous U.S., Mount Whitney. The vegetation and wildlife are diverse in Death Valley and include coyotes, bighorn sheep, creosote bushes, Joshua trees, and the Death Valley pupfish.

Best Time to Visit: The best time to visit is during the fall and winter when the weather isn't as hot.

Pass/Permit/Fees: There is a $30 fee per vehicle.

Closest City or Town: Death Valley, California

Physical Address:
Death Valley National Park Post Office
328 Greenland Boulevard
Furnace Creek, CA 92328

GPS Coordinates: 36.6827° N, 117.0848° W

Did You Know? Several Native American tribes lived in the Death Valley area as early as 7000 BC, including the Timbisha tribe.

Racetrack

One of the most famous Death Valley attractions, Racetrack, is named for the tracks left behind by stones that seemingly move on their own. Human or animal involvement was always out of the question, as the desolate lake bed, or playa, is largely undisturbed due to its remote location. Nicknamed the "sailing stones," the synchronized, linear tracks were a mystery until 2016. This geological phenomenon is only accessible via an all-day trek in a four-wheel-drive vehicle. After arriving at the north end of the Racetrack and Grandstand parking area, the short walk to the Grandstand can be rewarding. To see the rocks, drive two miles south of the Grandstand parking area and walk about half a mile toward the southeast of the playa.

Best Time to Visit: Visit between September and June.

Pass/Permit/Fees: There is a $25 fee per vehicle for seven days to visit the Racetrack in Death Valley.

Closest City or Town: Death Valley, California

Physical Address:
Death Valley National Park Post Office
328 Greenland Boulevard
Furnace Creek, CA 92328

GPS Coordinates: 36.6813° N, 117.5627° W

Did You Know? Some of the rocks in the playa weigh as much as 700 pounds.

Imperial Sand Dunes

Formed by windblown sands of the ancient Lake Cahuilla, the Imperial Sand Dunes are the largest mass of sand dunes in California. Reaching heights of 300 feet, the dune system extends for more than 40 miles in a band. The Imperial Sand Dunes Recreational Area (ISDRA) offers off-road action for vehicles, including fabulous scenery, solitude, and rare wildlife. There's also the North Algodones Dunes Wilderness, a tranquil location that encompasses 26,000 acres.

Best Time to Visit: Visit during the winter for moderate temperatures.

Pass/Permit/Fees: Permits are required to visit the Imperial Sand Dunes between October 1 and April 15. The permit fee is $35 per week in advance or $50 onsite.

Closest City or Town: El Centro, California

Physical Address:
El Centro Visitor Center
1275 W Main Street
El Centro, CA 92243

GPS Coordinates: 32.9734° N, 115.1727° W

Did You Know? The sand dunes have been featured in several movies, including *Star Wars: Return of the Jedi* and *Jumanji 3.*

Encinitas Meditation Gardens

The Encinitas Meditation Gardens provide a quiet, peaceful escape from the city with their colorful plants, koi ponds, ocean vistas, and meditation nooks. The activities are designed to connect visitors with the divinity within themselves. The gardens were designed in the 1930s by the founder of the Self-Realization Fellowship, Paramahansa Yogananda, following the founding of the international fellowship in 1920. The gardens comprise 17 acres and have inspired Encinitas' identity, including the golden lotus blossom-topped towers on Swami Beach, a favorite surf spot of locals and visitors alike.

Best Time to Visit: The best time to visit the gardens is during the spring and fall when the weather is milder.

Pass/Permit/Fees: There is no fee to visit the gardens.

Closest City or Town: Encinitas, California

Physical Address:
215 W K Street
Encinitas, CA 92024

GPS Coordinates: 33.0375° N, 117.2947° W

Did You Know? A highlight of the Meditation Gardens is a Monterey pine tree given to Yogananda as a gift. It is referred to as the "Ming Tree" or "Little Emperor" and is cut to resemble a large bonsai tree.

Founders Grove

Located along the Avenue of the Giants, Founders Grove is a half-mile hike full of luscious green moss and enormous redwood trees. The trees have grown incredibly tall due to the shelter provided by the 3,000-foot mountains to the west. The summer fog keeps the trees watered consistently, so any irregular rainfall is not an issue. The centerpiece of the grove is the Founders Tree, which is 346 feet tall, surpassing the height of the trees around it. There is a walk-up platform that allows visitors to get close and marvel at the massive size of this tree. Additionally, make sure to check out Hollow Tree, a standing tree you can walk into.

Best Time to Visit: The best time to visit Founders Grove is before 8 a.m. or during the winter.

Pass/Permit/Fees: There is no fee to visit Founders Grove.

Closest City or Town: Eureka, California

Physical Address:
Humboldt Redwoods State Park
17119 Avenue of the Giants
Weott, CA 95571

GPS Coordinates: 40.3513° N, 123.9273° W

Did You Know? The Dyersville Giant is a huge tree that fell in 1991. It is 370 feet long and believed to be 1,600 years old.

Redwood Forest National Park

One of three parks in the Redwood National and State Park System, this area is home to the tallest trees in the world. Hyperion, the world's largest tree, was discovered in 2006, located in a remote grove. It stands at 379.1 feet tall, making it six stories higher than the Statue of Liberty. There are ample places to camp at the developed campgrounds or the backcountry camps at this park. In addition, there are dozens of trails full of scenic routes.

Best Time to Visit: There is no inopportune time to visit the Redwood Forest National Park.

Pass/Permit/Fees: There is a $35 developed campground fee, and reservations are required. Free permits are required for backcountry camping (with the exception of Gold Bluffs Beach, $5 fee per person per night).

Closest City or Town: Eureka, California

Physical Address:
111 Second Street
Crescent City, CA 95531

GPS Coordinates: 41.2132° N, 124.0046° W

Did You Know? Redwood National and State Parks contain 45% of the remaining protected old-growth redwoods of California, spanning 38,000 acres.

Roaring Camp & Big Trees Narrow Gauge Railroad

Roaring Camp & Big Trees Narrow Gauge Railroad runs for 2.35 miles through redwood forests to the top of Bear Mountain. It offers rides on several steam engines, including the Redwood Forest Steam Train and the Santa Cruz Beach Train. These trains date from the 1890s and are some of the oldest narrow-gauge trains in the country. Roaring Camp Railroads was founded in 1963 by F. Norman Clark. The first engine was the Dixiana, which Clark found in 1958.

Best Time to Visit: The railroad runs all year.

Pass/Permit/Fees: Tickets for adults are $39.95 and $24.95 for children between the ages of two and 12. Children ages one and under can ride for free.

Closest City or Town: Felton, California

Physical Address:
5401 Graham Hill Road
Felton, CA 95018

GPS Coordinates: 37.0413° N, 122.0609° W

Did You Know? The switchback at Spring Canyon has an estimated 9.5% grade, which is the steepest passenger grade of any railroad still in use.

Folsom Lake

Located in the Sierra Nevada foothills, Folsom Lake is 11,500 acres in size and has 75 miles of shoreline. It is part of the Folsom Lake State Recreation Area and is one of the busiest in the entire California park system. Folsom Lake was created in 1955 when Folsom Dam was constructed to control the American River as part of the Central Valley Project, which was implemented to provide flood control, drinking water, hydroelectricity, and water for irrigation to surrounding communities. Activities like water-skiing, boating, fishing, and jet skiing make up 85% of all recreational visits to the park.

Best Time to Visit: The best times to visit Folsom Lake are spring and summer.

Pass/Permit/Fees: There is a $12 fee per vehicle to visit Folsom Lake.

Closest City or Town: Folsom, California

Physical Address:
7755 Folsom-Auburn Road
Folsom, CA 95630

GPS Coordinates: 38.7435° N, 121.1224° W

Did You Know? When the area where Folsom Lake is located was hit by a drought in 2013, the town of Mormon Island reappeared after 58 years of being underwater.

Glass Beach

Glass Beach was formed by humans and nature combined. In the early to mid-1900s, this site was used as a trash dump, which is where the glass originates. Over time, the ocean broke and flattened the glass into smooth, colorful pieces. The sea glass mixed in with the pebbles and sand to create Glass Beach. There are actually three beaches in the area that feature colorful, smooth sea glass. Unfortunately, the glass is frequently taken from the beach by visitors, although it is illegal to do so.

Best Time to Visit: The best time to visit Glass Beach is between June and October.

Pass/Permit/Fees: There is no fee to visit Glass Beach.

Closest City or Town: Fort Bragg, California

Physical Address:
MacKerricher State Park
24100 MacKerricher Park Road
Fort Bragg, CA 95437

GPS Coordinates: 39.4526° N, 123.8135° W

Did You Know? Glass Beach is thought to have the highest concentration of sea glass in the world.

Whiskeytown Falls

Widely recognized as one of the best waterfalls in Northern California, Whiskey Falls is a 220-foot high waterfall. It is reached via a strenuous 1.7 mile uphill hike on the James K. Carr Trail (3.4-mile round trip). The hike itself is beautiful and allows you to climb through dense forests and traverse over a few small bridges before arriving at the falls. Whiskeytown Falls is one of four waterfalls in the park and is the tallest and most visited. Shade is abundant, but it is very hot during the summer.

Best Time to Visit: The best times to visit Whiskeytown Falls are spring and early summer.

Pass/Permit/Fees: There is a $10 weekly fee to visit Whiskeytown Falls.

Closest City or Town: French Gulch, California

Physical Address:
Whiskeytown National Recreation Area
14412 Kennedy Memorial Drive
Whiskeytown, CA 96095

GPS Coordinates: 40.6264° N, 122.6692° W

Did You Know? Whiskey Falls was recently discovered by park managers of the Whiskeytown Recreation Area in 2004. Prior to that, the waterfalls were a local secret and had been mis-mapped.

General Grant Grove

Located in Kings Canyon National Park, General Grant Grove features giant sequoia trees. Its namesake tree, General Grant, is the second-largest tree in the world at 267 feet tall and 107 feet wide. The tree was named in 1867 after Ulysses S. Grant. Declared a National Shrine by President Eisenhower in 1956, General Grant Tree is the only example of a living shrine in the United States. There are several trail options to view the giant sequoias in the grove, including the General Grant Tree Trail.

Best Time to Visit: The best time to visit General Grant Grove is between June and August.

Pass/Permit/Fees: There is a $35 fee per vehicle, a $40 fee per motorcycle, or a $20 fee per individual on foot or bicycle.

Closest City or Town: Fresno, California

Physical Address:
Sequoia National Park
47050 Generals Highway
Three Rivers, CA 93271

GPS Coordinates: 36.7483° N, 118.9712° W

Did You Know? President Calvin Coolidge designated General Grant as the nation's Christmas tree on April 28, 1926.

Gray Whale Cove State Beach

Gray Whale Cove State Beach is a popular place to watch gray whales during their migratory journey in the winter. Also called Devil's Slide, Gray Whale Cove State Beach offers beachgoers a sheltered cove surrounded by steep cliffs that drop dramatically into the Pacific Ocean. From the parking lot on the east side of Highway 1, there is a steep trail that leads down to the beach, where there is also a picnic area. Be aware that this beach is well-known for its "clothing optional" policy, so take care before bringing children to the area.

Best Time to Visit: The best time to visit Gray Whale Cove State Beach is during the winter when gray whales migrate close to the shore.

Pass/Permit/Fees: There is no fee to visit.

Closest City or Town: Half Moon Bay, California

Physical Address:
Half Moon Bay Coastside Visitor Center
235 Main Street
Half Moon Bay, CA 94019

GPS Coordinates: 37.5652° N, 122.5139° W

Did You Know? There is a condemned World War II bunker directly above the north side of the beach that is closed to the public but makes for wonderful photographs.

36

Silverwood Lake

Silverwood Lake is a large reservoir that was created in 1971 to provide drinking water and hydroelectricity to surrounding communities. The lake is a popular destination for swimming, boating, water-skiing, and fishing. The Pacific Crest Trail, which is a 2,650-mile trail spanning from Canada to Mexico, passes through the Silverwood Lake State Recreation Area. There are trailheads for both short and long hikes. While the lake is also popular for fishing, a 2009 study concluded that there were elevated mercury levels in the largemouth bass in the lake, prompting an eating advisory for any fish caught from these waters.

Best Time to Visit: Visit during spring and summer, as the high elevation makes it bitterly cold in the fall and winter.

Pass/Permit/Fees: There is a $10 fee per vehicle to visit.

Closest City or Town: Hesperia, California

Physical Address:
14651 Cedar Circle
Hesperia, CA 92345

GPS Coordinates: 34.2997° N, 117.3242° W

Did You Know? The Cleghorn Swim Beach on the south point of Silverwood Lake is staffed with lifeguards throughout the summer and is an ideal place for kids.

Huntington Beach

Huntington Beach, also referred to as Surf City USA, is a seaside city in Orange County. Its 9.5-mile sandy beach, mild climate, and surf culture make it popular for both locals and tourists who want to experience a true, California-style beach. Surfers flock to the area because of the enhanced ocean waves that form due to a combination of Southern Hemisphere storms and swells originating in the North Pacific. This unique weather pattern creates consistently good waves for surfing all year long. =

Best Time to Visit: The best time to visit Huntington Beach is between September and November.

Pass/Permit/Fees: There is no fee to visit Huntington Beach.

Closest City or Town: Huntington Beach, California

Physical Address:
Huntington Beach Visitor Information Center
325 CA-1
Huntington Beach, CA 92648

GPS Coordinates: 33.6578° N, 118.0023° W

Did You Know? Not only is Huntington Beach well known for its spectacular surfing, but it also sits on top of a natural fault that contains oil, which is another major economic driver for the city.

Giant Rock in Landers

The Giant Rock in Landers is a seven-story giant boulder that is located in California's Mojave Desert. It covers nearly 6,000 square feet and maybe the largest free-standing boulder in the world. The giant rock has been a spiritual site for Native Americans for thousands of years, but in the 1930s, a German immigrant Frank Critzer built a 400-square-foot home directly beneath the rock. Critzer was a radio enthusiast and wanted to use the top of the rock for an antenna. However, during World War II, Critzer's German heritage and radio knowledge led the military to believe he was a spy, and he was killed when his home was raided.

Best Time to Visit: The best time to visit the Giant Rock in Landers is during the spring or fall to avoid the crowds.

Pass/Permit/Fees: There is no fee to visit.

Closest City or Town: Joshua Tree, California

Physical Address:
Joshua Tree Visitor Center
6554 Park Boulevard
Joshua Tree, CA 92252

GPS Coordinates: 34.3365° N, 116.3900° W

Did You Know? In the 1950s, the Giant Rock was a popular gathering point for people who believed in UFOs.

Bear Gulch Cave

Bear Gulch Cave is one of two unique caves in Pinnacles National Park. Bear Gulch and Balconies Caves were created by cave-ins rather than lava flows. Bear Gulch Cave is a talus cave that consists of open spaces among large rocks and boulders. There are a few converging trails around Bear Gulch, so watch your signs carefully at trail splits. Overall, it is a short and easy hike that takes you by beautiful rock formations and allows you to experience a unique talus cave.

Best Time to Visit: The best time to visit is mid-July through mid-May, depending on the presence of bats.

Pass/Permit/Fees: There is a $15 fee to visit Bear Gulch Cave.

Closest City or Town: King City, California

Physical Address:
Pinnacles National Park
5000 East Entrance Road
Paicines, CA 95043

GPS Coordinates: 40.8549° N, 122.7200° W

Did You Know? Bear Gulch Cave provides a home to a colony of Townsend's big-eared bats, a sensitive species.

Crystal Cove State Park

One of the most gorgeous coastlines in California, Laguna Beach is full of cliff formations, caves, rock arches, and tide pools. There are several amazing places to visit in this area, such as Crystal Cove. This state park features 3.2 miles of shoreline and 2,400 acres of backcountry wilderness. Mountain biking, horseback riding, and hiking are great activities on land, while divers can enjoy the underwater experience at the beach with tidepools and sandy coves, rocky reefs, ridges, and canyons. The scenic Moro Campground is available, and there are also 58 total sites for RVs, van conversions, and tents.

Best Time to Visit: The best time to visit Crystal Cove State Park is during the fall and winter, which is the off-season.

Pass/Permit/Fees: There is a $15 fee for parking.

Closest City or Town: Laguna Beach, California

Physical Address:
8471 N Coast Highway
Laguna Beach, CA 92651

GPS Coordinates: 33.5766° N, 117.8418° W

Did You Know? Crystal Cove is one of the largest remaining open spaces in Orange County, California.

Laguna Beach

Known for its mild climate, Laguna Beach is a popular seaside resort located in Orange County. With more than 6 million visitors each year, Laguna Beach attracts major annual events. The area has a well-established artist community of filmmakers, writers, painters, and photographers. In the 1960s and 1970s, Laguna Beach became California's epicenter for hippie culture. The Brotherhood of Eternal Love even relocated to the Woodland Drive neighborhood during this time.

Best Time to Visit: The best times to visit Laguna Beach are between April and May and between September and October. There are fewer tourists during these months, and the weather is milder than in the summer months.

Pass/Permit/Fees: There is no fee to visit Laguna Beach.

Closest City or Town: Laguna Beach, California

Physical Address:
Laguna Beach Visitors Center
381 Forest Avenue
Laguna Beach, CA 92651

GPS Coordinates: 33.5445° N, 117.7820° W

Did You Know? Laguna Beach is internationally known for mountain biking. Pioneers of mountain biking, Hans Rey and the Rads, make their home in the area.

Antelope Valley Poppy Reserve

The state-protected Antelope Valley Poppy Reserve features the most consistently blooming fields of California poppies in the country. The blooming season usually occurs as early as mid-February, but it is dependent upon the amount of rainfall the region receives during the winter. There are seven miles of hiking trails, including a paved trail that provides wheelchair access through the poppy fields. The reserve is maintained in a strictly natural state, so the poppies are not watered or otherwise artificially stimulated by the California State Parks department. Additionally, the fields are protected from grazing animals to ensure their regrowth.

Best Time to Visit: The best time to visit Antelope Valley Poppy Reserve is in early spring (mid-February to mid-March).

Pass/Permit/Fees: There is no fee to visit the poppy fields.

Closest City or Town: Lancaster, California

Physical Address:
15101 Lancaster Road
Lancaster, CA 93536

GPS Coordinates: 34.7257° N, 118.3968° W

Did You Know? The poppy is the state flower of California.

Vasquez Rocks

Vasquez Rocks is an area full of spectacular rock formations that span 932 acres. Earthquakes from the San Andreas Fault have twisted and folded the rocks into jagged, sharp shapes and strange angles. This landscape is legendary and has been the backdrop for multiple Hollywood movies. The Vasquez Rocks Natural Area features several trails, with the main attraction of Famous Rocks found at the heart of the park. There are several possible routes that can get you to the Famous Rocks, with various extensions to traverse if you want to explore the area. The Pacific Crest Trail is the ideal place to start.

Best Time to Visit: The shadows of Vasquez Rocks are beautifully dramatic and best witnessed during either the morning in summer or the afternoon in winter.

Pass/Permit/Fees: There is no fee to visit Vasquez Rocks.

Closest City or Town: Lancaster, California

Physical Address:
10700 Escondido Canyon Road
Agua Dulce, CA 91390

GPS Coordinates: 34.4885° N, 118.3207° W

Did You Know? The park is named after a famous bandit, Tiburcio Vasquez, who evaded law enforcement by hiding in this area.

Mono Lake

Mono Lake is an ancient saline lake famous for its tufa towers. Tufas are soft, porous rock formations, and their towers form beneath Mono Lake in the calcium-rich springs that seep up into the water's bottom. The calcium comes into contact with the carbonites in the lake, and a chemical reaction occurs, resulting in limestone. The lake water is incredibly dense because of the high salt content. Due to the brine shrimp and alkali flies, Mono Lake draws flocks of birds. The tufa towers standing along the shoreline of the lake make for great photos. Visitors can also kayak on the lake.

Best Time to Visit: The best time to visit Mono Lake is between December and March.

Pass/Permit/Fees: There is a $10 fee to visit Mono Lake.

Closest City or Town: Lee Vining, California

Physical Address:
Mono Lake Tufa State Natural Reserve Visitor Center
Lee Vining Creek Trail
Lee Vining, CA 93541

GPS Coordinates: 38.0128° N, 118.9762° W

Did You Know? Tufas here reach heights of 15 to 20 feet above water and over 30 feet underwater.

Fossil Falls

Fossil Falls is a bit of a misnomer since there aren't any fossils or waterfalls. However, thousands of years ago, the Owens River flowed through the Coso Range area and interacted with lava from nearby volcanoes, creating the "falls" that are actually sculpted black lava rocks. Glaciers also played a role in shaping this unique area. The trail to the falls is only 0.2 miles and full of volcanic rock. The falls themselves are barren, so while you won't be looking for water, be on the lookout for a rather strange rock cluster that was once a waterfall. The rock gives way to a 60–70-foot drop through a volcanic rock canyon that experienced climbers love. The short trail leads you to observe the falls from above, and there is also a trail to descend the falls. Be wary of loose rocks on the descending trail.

Best Time to Visit: Visit during the fall or spring.

Pass/Permit/Fees: There is no fee to visit Fossil Falls.

Closest City or Town: Little Lake, California

Physical Address:
Ridgecrest Area Convention & Visitors Bureau
880 N China Lake Road
Ridgecrest, CA 93555

GPS Coordinates: 35.9699° N, 117.9090° W

Did You Know? This desert location makes for spectacular views of the night sky.

Livermore Valley Wine Country

Located a few miles from the California Coast, directly east of the San Francisco Bay, Livermore Valley Wine Country is home to more than 50 wineries. The first vineyards were planted in the early 1880s by pioneer winemakers C.H. Wente and James Concannon. Both men still have descendants in the area who continue to make wine. The region boasts 2,000 vineyard hectares and produces approximately 80% of California's chardonnay.

Best Time to Visit: The best time to visit Livermore Valley Wine Country is between May and August when the vineyards are in bloom.

Pass/Permit/Fees: Tasting and touring fees vary by winery. Contact the specific winery you want to visit for rates.

Closest City or Town: Livermore, California

Physical Address:
Livermore Valley Winegrowers Association
3585 Greenville Road, Suite 4
Livermore, CA 94550

GPS Coordinates: 37.6757° N, 121.6982° W

Did You Know? More than 30 varietals are grown in Livermore Valley.

Mobius Arch

Mobius Arch is found in Alabama Hills Recreation Area, a site where many cowboy movies have been filmed. The arch is a circular rock formation that is large, unique, and surrounded by beautiful geological formations. The window of the arch is about 6.5 feet high and perfectly frames Mt. Whitney when viewed from the correct angle.

The Mobius Arch Loop Trail is only 0.6 miles and easy to travel, as it's well-marked with brown posts and stone. The drive from Lone Pine is short, making Mobius Arch an ideal stop if you are on the way to other sites in the area, such as Mt. Whitney. After Mobius Arch, there is a trail to Lathe Arch if you're feeling adventurous.

Best Time to Visit: The best time to visit Mobius Arch is between May and October.

Pass/Permit/Fees: There is no fee to visit Mobius Arch.

Closest City or Town: Lone Pine, California

Physical Address:
US-395 and CA-136
Lone Pine, CA 93545

GPS Coordinates: 36.6113° N, 118.1249° W

Did You Know? Mobius Arch got its name from the way it folds over, like a Mobius strip.

Mount Whitney

Mt. Whitney is the tallest peak in the 48 states and offers a grand view of the Sierra Nevada Mountains. However, since Mt. Whitney is on the eastern boundary of Sequoia National Park, there is a chain of mountains through the center that blocks views of Whitney from park roads. A good view can be seen at the Interagency Visitor Center on Hwy. 395. Adventurers can also climb the mountain from the west in Sequoia National Park or from the east in Inyo National Forest. Most people climb from the east side, as the shortest and most popular route begins from Whitney Portal, 13 miles west of Lone Pine, California.

Best Time to Visit: The best time to visit Mount Whitney is between July and October.

Pass/Permit/Fees: Permits are required for hiking and backpacking from May 1st-November 1st and are distributed via lottery. The fee is $6 per application and $15 per person.

Closest City or Town: Lone Pine, California

Physical Address:
US-395 and CA-136
Lone Pine, CA 93545

GPS Coordinates: 36.5785° N, 118.2923° W

Did You Know? The summit offers stunning views of Death Valley National Park.

Griffith Park

With 4,210 acres of park and natural area, Griffith Park is one of the largest municipal parks that includes an urban wilderness in the U.S. The vegetation is very diverse, including oak trees, walnut trees, lilac bushes, mountain mahogany trees, sages, toyon, and sumac. You'll also find small samples of berberis and manzanita, both of which are threatened species. You can visit the Autry Museum of the American West, the Bronson Caves, the Greek Theatre, a merry-go-round, the Griffith Observatory, the Southern Railroad, the L.A. Equestrian Center, the Los Angeles Zoo, Travel Town, and more.

Best Time to Visit: The best time to visit Griffith Park is any time of the year during the mornings to avoid crowds.

Pass/Permit/Fees: There is no fee to visit Griffith Park, but individual attractions set their own rates.

Closest City or Town: Los Angeles, California

Physical Address:
4730 Crystal Springs Drive
Los Angeles, CA 90027

GPS Coordinates: 34.1374° N, 118.2943° W

Did You Know? Griffith Park is named for its original owner, Colonel Griffith J. Griffith, an Englishman who emigrated to the U.S. in 1865.

Los Angeles County Museum of Art

The Los Angeles County Museum of Art was established in 1961. It is located on Wilshire Boulevard in what is known as "Miracle Mile." As the largest art museum in the western United States, the museum attracts almost a million visitors each year and has a collection of over 150,000 works of art, encompassing all eras of history. Additionally, the museum hosts concert series, film screenings, and various educational programs.

Best Time to Visit: The Los Angeles County Museum of Art is open Monday, Tuesday, and Thursday from 11:00 a.m. to 6:00 p.m., Friday from 11:00 a.m. to 8:00 p.., and Saturday and Sunday from 10:00 a.m. to 7:00 p.m.

Pass/Permit/Fees: Admission ranges between $20 to $25 per adult, $0 to $10 for teens aged 13 through 17, and $16 to $21 for seniors aged 65 and older.

Closest City or Town: Los Angeles, California

Physical Address:
5905 Wilshire Boulevard
Los Angeles, CA 90036

GPS Coordinates: 34.0648° N, 118.3590° W

Did You Know? The Los Angeles County Museum of Art hosts an annual fundraising Art + Film Gala that brings in about $4.5 million a year for operations and collections.

Santa Catalina Island

Santa Catalina Island is a rocky mass of land located off the southern coast of California. It is about 22 miles long and measures 8 miles at its widest point. Throughout its history, Catalina Island was home to several Southern California Native American Tribes. After the Spanish Empire claimed the island, it was used for smuggling, gold-digging, otter hunting and was developed for tourism in the 1920s.

Best Time to Visit: Visit the island during the spring and fall, when the weather is calm and warm.

Pass/Permit/Fees: There is no fee to visit Santa Catalina Island, but there is a fee to take the ferry from San Pedro or Long Beach. An adult fare ranges from $38 one way to $76 round trip, the fare for children between the ages of two and 11 ranges between $30.25 and $60.50, and the fare for seniors aged 55 and older ranges between $34.50 and $69.

Closest City or Town: Los Angeles, California

Physical Address:
Catalina Island Visitor Center
1 Green Pleasure Pier
Avalon, CA 90704

GPS Coordinates: 33.4208° N, 118.4138° W

Did You Know? Santa Catalina Island was used as a military training base during World War II.

The Getty Center Los Angeles

As part of the Getty Museum, the Getty Center Los Angeles is a museum that is home to a wonderful collection of art from Cezanne, Van Gogh, and Monet. It is also well-known for its architecture, gardens, and spectacular views of Los Angeles. The Getty Center is located in the Brentwood neighborhood and is one of two locations that make up the J. Paul Getty Museum. More than 1.8 million visitors come to these two facilities each year. The Getty Center was designed by architect Richard Meier and is also home to the Getty Research Institute, the Getty Foundation, the Getty Conservation Institute, and the J. Paul Getty Trust.

Best Time to Visit: The Getty Center Los Angeles is open daily from 10:00 a.m. to 5:30 p.m.

Pass/Permit/Fees: There is no fee to visit the Getty Center Los Angeles.

Closest City or Town: Los Angeles, California

Physical Address:
1200 Getty Center Drive
Los Angeles, CA 90049

GPS Coordinates: 34.0786° N, 118.4741° W

Did You Know? The original museum, which opened in 1954, was housed in J. Paul Getty's house.

53

Universal Studios Hollywood

This combination of film studio and theme park is one of the oldest and most well-known studios in Hollywood. The theme park was initially created to provide tours of Universal Studios to visitors but soon evolved to be one of the first of several full-fledged theme parks around the world. Visitors will enjoy an immersive experience and recognize many favorite productions.

Best Time to Visit: Universal Studios Hollywood is open Monday through Friday from 9:00 a.m. to 7:00 p.m. and Saturday and Sunday from 9:00 a.m. to 8:00 p.m.

Pass/Permit/Fees: Ticket prices to visit Universal Studios Hollywood vary but range between $110 to $125 per adult and $104 to $119 per child.

Closest City or Town: Los Angeles, California

Physical Address:
100 Universal City Plaza
Universal City, CA 91608

GPS Coordinates: 34.1390° N, 118.3531° W

Did You Know? Universal Studios Hollywood has been damaged by fire nine times since its opening in 1915, the worst of which was in 2008.

Malibu

Malibu is a famous beach city located in Los Angeles County. It is best known for its mild Mediterranean climate and its 21-mile coastline. The Malibu Colony has been home to numerous Hollywood celebrities and other affluent residents. Surfers have nicknamed the area "the Bu" and enjoy the many beaches, including Topanga Beach, Surfrider Beach, Zuma Beach, Point Dume Beach, and others. Malibu is also home to the Getty Villa, an art museum that is an extension of the J. Paul Getty Museum and the Adamson House, a historic home and garden that once belonged to the original owners of Malibu.

Best Time to Visit: The best time to visit Malibu is between June and September, especially for surfing.

Pass/Permit/Fees: There is no fee to visit Malibu.

Closest City or Town: Malibu, California

Physical Address:
Malibu Visitor Center
35000 Pacific Highway W
Malibu, CA 90265

GPS Coordinates: 34.0469° N, 118.9340° W

Did You Know? Malibu's name comes from the Native American Ventureno Chumash settlement Humaliwo, which means "the surf sounds loudly."

Devils Postpile

Located near Mammoth Mountain is the geologic wonder, Devils Postpile. This formation is a rare sight of massive rocks that seemingly jut out of the earth's surface. It is one of the world's finest examples of columnar basalt, and the columns tower up to 60 feet and measure 2-3.5 feet in diameter. These unique rock formations are hexagonal at the top, which can be viewed up close as a part of the hike. Devils Postpile Trail is full of beautiful views, and once there, you have the option to continue to Rainbow Falls. Since 1911, the area has been protected as a national monument.

Best Time to Visit: Visit between June and October.

Pass/Permit/Fees: There is an $8 fee for a day pass, a $16 fee for a three-day pass, or a $40 fee for a season pass.

Closest City or Town: Mammoth Lakes, California

Physical Address:
Mammoth Lakes Welcome Center
2510 Main Street
Mammoth Lakes, CA 93546

GPS Coordinates: 37.6251° N, 119.0850° W

Did You Know? The hexagonal columns are believed to have formed 10,000 years ago from a cliff of cooled lava.

Mammoth Lakes Basin

Mammoth Lakes Basin consists of numerous glacier-carved lakes, including Lake Mary, Lake George, Twin Lakes, Lake Mamie, and Horseshoe Lake. Popular water activities include boating, kayaking, paddle boarding, and fishing. On-shore activities include biking, hiking, backpacking, and in the winter, snowshoeing. Anglers love the area because there are many fish species in the lakes, including rainbow trout, brown trout, brook trout, golden trout, perch, smallmouth bass, and Owens sucker (a fish that is native only to California).

Best Time to Visit: The best time to visit Mammoth Lakes Basin is during the summer for water activities and during the winter for snowshoeing.

Pass/Permit/Fees: There is a $15 fee per person.

Closest City or Town: Mammoth Lakes, California

Physical Address:
Mammoth Lakes Welcome Center
2500 Main Street
Mammoth Lakes, CA 93546

GPS Coordinates: 37.6156° N, 119.0215° W

Did You Know? Mammoth Lakes sits on the edge of a 20-mile-wide extinct supervolcano that erupted approximately 750,000 years ago.

Mammoth Mountain

Due to its location in the Sierra Crest, Mammoth Mountain gets an unusually large amount of snowfall and is home to the Mammoth Mountain Ski Area. During the winter months, visitors can ski, snowboard, and snowmobile at the highest ski resort in California. It is a four-season resort, so the summer offers activities of its own, including guided climbing, mountain biking, and scenic trails. The gondola operates throughout the year and is a perfect opportunity for aerial views and a ride to the summit.

Best Time to Visit: The best time to visit depends on the activities you want to participate in.

Pass/Permit/Fees: There is no fee to visit Mammoth Mountain, but ski lift tickets are between $30-$80.

Closest City or Town: Mammoth Lakes, California

Physical Address:
Mammoth Mountain Ski Area
10001 Minaret Road
Mammoth Lakes, CA 93546

GPS Coordinates: 37.6308° N, 119.0326° W

Did You Know? At 11,059 feet in elevation, Mammoth Mountain is a lava dome complex, which means it has a circular mound shape formed from a series of volcanic eruptions around 60,000 years ago.

Thousand Island Lake

Thousand Island Lake is located in the Sierra Nevada Mountains and is a large alpine lake named for the numerous rocky islands that are scattered across its surface. It sits at the base of Banner Peak, which towers 12,936 feet above the lake's west shore. There are several trails that lead to the lake from Agnew Meadows, including the High Trail (part of the Pacific Crest Trail) and the John Muir Trail. The Lake has been described as a real-life postcard: a glassy blue lake that perfectly reflects Banner Peak, broken only by the small islands peaking up from the water.

Best Time to Visit: The best time to visit Thousand Island Lake is during August when the weather is still warm but the mosquitos are gone.

Pass/Permit/Fees: There is no fee to visit.

Closest City or Town: Mammoth Lakes, California

Physical Address:
Mammoth Lakes Welcome Center
2510 Main Street
Mammoth Lakes, CA 93546

GPS Coordinates: 37.7236° N, 119.1832° W

Did You Know? Famed black and white photographer Ansel Adams photographed Thousand Island Lake numerous times, making it a Sierra Nevada landmark.

Painted Canyon

The Ladder Canyon Trail is a 4.5-mile loop that passes through a slot canyon, goes up a ridge, and leads you along the bottom of Big Painted Canyon. This is a two to three-hour trek, so be sure to take some water. Additionally, the trail surface is comprised of sand and loose gravel coupled with climbing ladders, so getting to Painted Canyon will take some effort. However, once you reach the top, the views are amazing, and the canyons are beautiful. The trail also features a waterfall and is rated as moderate.

Best Time to Visit: The best time to visit Painted Canyon is between October and April.

Pass/Permit/Fees: There is no fee to visit Painted Canyon.

Closest City or Town: Mecca, California

Physical Address:
Painted Canyon Trailhead
Painted Canyon Rd
Mecca, CA 92254

GPS Coordinates: 33.6192° N, 115.9994° W

Did You Know? The colorful walls of the exposed rock layers of the canyon include pink, red, gray, brown, and green.

Salton Sea

The Salton Sea is a saltwater lake located in Riverside that was formed by the Colorado River flowing into the valley over millions of years. In 1580, the river diverted around the valley and the lake dried up entirely.. In 1905, the river started flowing through the valley again and created the current lake. The area around the Salton Sea became a resort destination in the 1950s and 1960s, and birdwatching became the foremost activity since the wetlands are a major resting stop along the Pacific Flyway. There is currently an environmental project underway to preserve the lake and create ponds and wetlands along the shore to also protect the wildlife populations.

Best Time to Visit: The best time to visit Salton Sea is from October to June, when the weather is more temperate.

Pass/Permit/Fees: There is a $7 fee per person to visit.

Closest City or Town: Mecca, California

Physical Address:
100-225 State Park Road
Mecca, CA 92254

GPS Coordinates: 33.3816° N, 115.8504° W

Did You Know? The Salton Sea has a greater salinity than the Pacific Ocean at 44 grams of salt per liter of water.

Bowling Ball Beach

Located in Schooner Gulch State Beach, Bowling Ball Beach is named for the large round rocks that line the area, resembling giant bowling balls. These rock formations are only visible during low tide, so if you visit, be sure to check the tide charts before heading out. Bowling Ball Beach is a popular location for photographers, especially at sunset. There are also two trails that lead from the parking lot, one of which leads to the beach and one of which leads to the main Schooner Gulch Beach. If you're an avid surfer, Whiskey Shoals is a surfing area at the north end of Bowling Ball Beach and is popular for its consistent waves.

Best Time to Visit: The best time to visit Bowling Ball Beach is in the spring or summer during low tide.

Pass/Permit/Fees: There is no fee to visit.

Closest City or Town: Mendocino, California

Physical Address:
Ford House Visitor Center & Museum
45035 Main Street
Mendocino, CA 95460

GPS Coordinates: 38.8734° N, 123.6590° W

Did You Know? The "bowling balls" are actually concretions that were eroded by the Pacific Ocean over millions of years.

Mendocino Coast

The Mendocino Coast stretches for more than 90 miles along the Pacific Ocean. The coast extends from Sonoma to Humboldt County, with many hidden beaches tucked into the coves and rocky cliffs. While these beaches are often secluded, swimming is highly discouraged because the currents and rocky terrain can be extremely dangerous. The pristine, wild coastline beckons artists and nature lovers, and the city of Mendocino itself resembles a New England village with saltbox cottages and white picket fences.

Best Time to Visit: The best time to visit the Mendocino Coast is during the winter months since it is the height of the whale-watching season.

Pass/Permit/Fees: There is no fee to visit the Mendocino Coast, but some beaches may have separate entrance fees.

Closest City or Town: Mendocino, California

Physical Address:
Ford House Visitor Center & Museum
45035 Main Street
Mendocino, CA 95460

GPS Coordinates: 39.3052° N, 123.7998 W

Did You Know? Mendocino was a logging town through the late 1800s before becoming a tourist city with boutique B&Bs, fancy restaurants, and fine art museums.

Half Dome

Perhaps the most recognizable landmark in Yosemite National Park, Half Dome is a granite dome formation found at the eastern end of Yosemite Valley. The sheer vertical face of one side starkly contrasts with the rounded dome and is viewable from several vantage points around the national park. You can only climb Half Dome when the cables are up. The entire Half Dome trail is 17 miles round trip, and it rises 4,737 feet above the floor of the valley.

Best Time to Visit: Visit Half Dome between May and October if you plan on climbing.

Pass/Permit/Fees: Cable route permits are awarded via lottery. Entering the lottery costs $10 and covers six permits per application. Winners pay an additional $10 per person. Visitors also pay the park's entrance fee: $30 in summer and $25 in winter.

Closest City or Town: Merced, California

Physical Address:
Yosemite National Park
7403 Yosemite Park Way
Yosemite National Park, CA 95389

GPS Coordinates: 37.7459° N, 119.5332° W

Did You Know? The first ascent of Half Dome was done by George G. Anderson in 1875.

Bumpass Hell

Appropriately named, Bumpass Hell consists of 16 acres of boiling springs, mud pots, fumaroles, and steam vents. This is the most popular geothermal area in Lassen Volcanic National Park. Bumpass Hell contains Big Boiler, the biggest fumarole in the park and one of the hottest in the world. The colorful soil and fool's gold are interesting to see, and the 2.6-mile round-trip trail is scenic. Just make sure you prepare for the smell of sulfur once you arrive at the otherworldly landscape of Bumpass Hell.

Best Time to Visit: The best time to visit Bumpass Hell is during the summer or fall.

Pass/Permit/Fees: There is a $30 fee per vehicle, or $25 per motorcycle, to enter Lassen Volcanic National Park.

Closest City or Town: Mineral, California

Physical Address:
Lassen Volcanic National Park
38050 Highway 36 East
Mineral, CA 96063

GPS Coordinates: 40.4582° N, 121.5011° W

Did You Know? The striking soil colors occur due to the minerals in the water, with orange and yellow soil contrasting starkly against bright blue and emerald green water.

17 Mile Drive

Along 17 Mile Drive, you'll view dramatic coastal cliffs, dense forests, iconic golf courses, and white sandy beaches. As one of the most scenic drives in the world, you'll marvel at the natural beauty of Fanshell Beach, the Restless Sea at Point Joe, and the boardwalk and beach of Spanish Bay. 17 Mile Drive has been open to the public as a scenic byway since 1881. While you drive along this incredible route, be sure to visit the Lone Cypress!

Best Time to Visit: The drive is gorgeous year-round.

Pass/Permit/Fees: There is a $10.75 fee per vehicle to drive along 17 Mile Drive, but it can be reimbursed with any purchase of $35 or more at any Pebble Beach Resorts restaurant (except Pebble Beach Market).

Closest City or Town: Monterey, California

Physical Address:
Monterey County Convention & Visitors Bureau
419 Webster Street, Suite 100
Monterey, CA 93940

GPS Coordinates: 36.5738° N, 121.9488° W

Did You Know? Plan to spend three hours for the whole drive because you'll definitely want to take pictures and walk around.

Monterey Bay Aquarium

The Monterey Bay Aquarium offers visitors unique exhibits featuring everything from sea otters to seaweed. In the Monterey Bay Aquarium's quest to inspire ocean conservation, its scientists are in the process of rebuilding sea otter populations, working to protect California's ocean, transforming worldwide fisheries and aquaculture, and proposing legislation to end plastic pollution and address climate change. Since 1984, the aquarium has also provided free admission to more than 2.5 million students to educate them on ocean conservation issues.

Best Time to Visit: The Monterey Bay Aquarium is open daily from 10:00 a.m. to 5:00 p.m.

Pass/Permit/Fees: Adult admission to visit the Monterey Bay Aquarium is $49.95. Youth admission (ages 13-17) is $39.95, child admission (ages 5-12) is $34.95, and senior admission (ages 65+) is $39.95.

Closest City or Town: Monterey, California

Physical Address:
886 Cannery Row
Monterey, CA 93940

GPS Coordinates: 36.6185° N, 121.9018° W

Did You Know? The Monterey Bay Aquarium features more than 200 exhibits and 80,000 plants and animals.

Monterey Beach

Monterey, California, was once the capital of Alta California under Spain from 1804 to 1821 and Mexico from 1822 to 1846. As a result, Monterey was home to California's first theatre, public building, public library, public school, printing press, and newspaper. It also hosted the state's first constitutional convention in 1849. Today, Monterey is an artist's paradise, attracting artistic types since the late 19th century. As a result, Monterey hosts many festivals and is home to famous creators, including John Steinbeck, Arthur Frank Mathews, Robert Louis Stevenson, Percy Gray, and others.

Best Time to Visit: The best time to visit Monterey Beach is between April and May, when the festivals are held.

Pass/Permit/Fees: There is no fee to visit Monterey Beach.

Closest City or Town: Monterey, California

Physical Address:
Monterey Visitors Information Center
401 Camino El Estero
Monterey, CA 93940

GPS Coordinates: 36.6153 N, 121.8583° W

Did You Know? The Monterey Jazz Festival got its start in 1958 and is now described as the "longest-running jazz festival in the world."

Morro Rock

Located in Morro Bay, this state historic landmark was formed around 23 million years ago from an extinct volcano. Morro Rock is a volcanic plug at the entrance to Morro Bay Harbor. The rock is located near Morro Rock Beach, with additional six miles of unspoiled beaches to enjoy. You can drive to the base of Morro Rock, but climbing it is prohibited by law. There are various recreational activities to do while you're in Morro Bay, including oceanside golf, sailing, kayaking, hiking, fishing, whale watching, biking, surfing, and birdwatching. The Cloisters Wetland loop trail offers scenic views on your way to the rock.

Best Time to Visit: There is no inopportune time to visit Morro Rock.

Pass/Permit/Fees: There is no fee to visit Morro Rock.

Closest City or Town: Morro Bay

Physical Address:
Morro Bay Visitor Center
595 Harbor Street
Morro Bay, CA 93442

GPS Coordinates: 35.3694° N, 120.8677° W

Did You Know? The rock is about 576 feet tall and is the most visible in the chain of extinct volcanoes called the Nine Sisters.

Lake Berryessa

As the largest lake in Napa County, Lake Berryessa offers numerous recreational activities, including jet-skiing, water-skiing, fishing, kayaking, and canoeing. In fact, Lake Berryessa is one of the most popular locations in the U.S. for water-skiing enthusiasts, who refer to the part of the reservoir near the Monticello Dam as "the narrows." Another favorite activity at this lake is fishing for species such as largemouth bass, channel catfish, spotted bass, bullhead catfish, white catfish, carp, Crappie, bluegill, Sacramento pikeminnow, rainbow trout, brown trout, and brook trout, among others. On-shore activities include hiking, bicycling, picnicking, bird-watching, and swimming.

Best Time to Visit: While Lake Berryessa is excellent year-round, the best times to visit are spring and summer.

Pass/Permit/Fees: There is a $5 fee per vehicle to visit.

Closest City or Town: Napa, California

Physical Address:
5520 Knoxville Road
Napa, CA 94558

GPS Coordinates: 38.6258° N, 122.2533° W

Did You Know? Before the area was settled by Europeans, the area was home to the Pomo Native American tribe.

Napa Valley

Home to over 400 wineries, Napa Valley is one of the most famous wine regions in the world. Thomas Rutherford established himself as a grower and producer of wines in the 1870s and 1880s. The first commercial winery in the United States was opened in 1859 by John Patchett in what would eventually become part of Napa Valley. Charles Krug, an apprentice for Patchett, founded his own winery in the valley in 1861.

Best Time to Visit: is August through October for the harvest or March through May to avoid crowds.

Pass/Permit/Fees: There is no fee to visit Napa Valley, but each winery sets its own rates for wine tasting, tours, and other events.

Closest City or Town: Napa, California

Physical Address:
Napa Valley Welcome Center
1300 1st Street, #313
Napa, CA 94559

GPS Coordinates: 38.5061° N, 122.2607° W

Did You Know? While Chardonnay and Cabernet Sauvignon are the most widely planted grapes in Napa Valley, there are more than three dozen wine grape varieties found in the region.

Newport Beach

Once a hub for maritime industries like shipbuilding, boatbuilding, and commercial fishing, Newport Beach, is a coastal city located in Orange County and known for its sandy beaches. The only commercial operations today are ferries to Catalina Island, tours of the harbor, sport fishing, and whale-watching day trips. Newport Harbor is a major destination for all types of boating activities, such as sailing, rowing, fishing, kayaking, canoeing, and paddleboarding. There are also two popular farmers' markets in Newport Beach: one is in Corona Del Mar on Saturday mornings, and the other is in Lido Village on Sunday mornings.

Best Time to Visit: The best time to visit is May through November, especially if you want to go whale watching.

Pass/Permit/Fees: There is no fee to visit Newport Beach.

Closest City or Town: Newport Beach, California

Physical Address:
Newport Beach Tourist Information Center
1600 Newport Center Drive, #120
Newport Beach, CA 92660

GPS Coordinates: 33.6169° N, 117.8801° W

Did You Know? Newport Beach hosts the largest sailboat race in the world.

Ojai Valley

A noted tourist destination in Ventura County, the Ojai Valley is bustling with boutique hotels, recreation opportunities, and a large farmers' market. There are also numerous independent businesses that specialize in art, home improvement, and design. In fact, chain stores are prohibited by city ordinance to encourage local business development. On weekends, visitors are likely to find festivals, car shows, and art exhibitions on display throughout its streets. The Ojai Music Festival and the Ojai Playwrights Conference are two major events that occur annually in the valley.

Best Time to Visit: The best time to visit is during the spring, when the major festivals are usually scheduled.

Pass/Permit/Fees: There is no fee to visit Ojai Valley.

Closest City or Town: Ojai, California

Physical Address:
Ojai Visitors Center
150 W Ojai Avenue
Ojai, CA 93023

GPS Coordinates: 34.4488° N, 119.2701° W

Did You Know? The Ojai name is taken from the Mexican-era Rancho Ojai, but the city calls itself "Shangri-La" because of its natural beauty and focus on spirituality.

Subway Cave

Volcanic rock burst out 20,000 years ago to create Hat Creek Lava Flow. Exposed to the air above ground, the top of the lava flow cooled and solidified, but molten rock continued to flow and create a lava tube. The molten lava has long since drained away, allowing visitors to walk through the lava tube. Subway Cave is a section of that lava tube located between two areas where the ceiling caved in and is accessed via a metal staircase. The cave is located on the self-guided Subway Cave Trail, a 0.75-mile loop. It is cool and dark in the cave, so make sure to bring a flashlight and jacket and take note of the jagged ground.

Best Time to Visit: The best time to visit Subway Cave is between May and October. It is closed between November and April.

Pass/Permit/Fees: There is no fee to visit Subway Cave.

Closest City or Town: Old Station, California

Physical Address:
Lassen Volcanic National Park
38050 Highway 36 East
Mineral, CA 96063

GPS Coordinates: 40.6866° N, 121.4207° W

Did You Know? The opening to the cave begins before the descent and is called "Devil's Kitchen."

The Painted Dunes

Lassen Volcanic National Park is home to the Painted Dunes, a landscape that looks like a watercolor painting. One of nature's masterpieces, the sand has red and orange blotches, speckled with trees and offset by the black volcanic rock. The Painted Dunes are pumice fields that formed when the area's volcanoes released layers of volcanic ash, which oxidized after falling on the lava flow while still hot. The summit on top of Cinder Cone offers the best view of the landscape, but it is a challenging climb because of loose rocks.

Best Time to Visit: The best times to visit the Painted Dunes are during the summer and fall.

Pass/Permit/Fees: There is a $30 fee per vehicle, $25 fee per motorcycle, or $15 fee per individual to visit the dunes.

Closest City or Town: Old Station, California

Physical Address:
Lassen Volcanic National Park
38050 Highway 36 East
Mineral, CA 96063

GPS Coordinates: 31.9565° N, 106.4046° W

Did You Know? Lassen Volcanic National Park is one of the few places in the world that contains all four types of volcanoes.

Fern Canyon

Fern Canyon is a narrow canyon lined with lush green ferns, mosses, and Home Creek running through its middle. Located in the Prairie Creek Redwoods State Park, Fern Canyon is well-known for its 50-foot-high, towering plant walls. An easy 1.1-mile hike takes you through coastal forests and to hidden waterfalls. Keep in mind that this is a wet journey, so wear shoes suitable for water. Depending on the time of year, you should also be cautious of Roosevelt Elk.

Best Time to Visit: The best time to visit Fern Canyon is June through September, when the creek isn't as high, but the greenery is still luscious.

Pass/Permit/Fees: There is an $8 cash-only park entrance fee.

Closest City or Town: Orick, California

Physical Address:
Prairie Creek Redwoods State Park
127011 Newton B. Drury Scenic Parkway
Orick, CA 9555

GPS Coordinates: 41.4016° N, 124.0650° W

Did You Know? Steven Spielberg chose Fern Canyon as a filming spot for *Jurassic Park 2*.

76

Oxnard Beach Park

This family-friendly beach is situated between Oxnard Shores and the Embassy Suites Resort. It not only features a white sandy beach with incredible views of Channel Island National Park, but it also has plenty of green space, free public barbecue areas, a kids play area, volleyball courts, skating paths, and jogging paths. It's a popular place for bicyclists to stop and rest when they're commuting through the area. There is even a pirate ship jungle gym on the kids' playground!

Best Time to Visit: The best time to visit Oxnard Beach Park is during the spring or summer.

Pass/Permit/Fees: There is a $5 cash-only fee per vehicle per day to visit Oxnard Beach Park.

Closest City or Town: Oxnard, California

Physical Address:
1601 S. Harbor Boulevard
Oxnard, CA 93035

GPS Coordinates: 34.1831° N, 119.2368° W

Did You Know? Oxnard Beach Park is located along the Pacific Coast Bicycle Route and the California Coast Trail, making it a popular connection point for several communities.

Mount San Jacinto

Standing at 10,084 feet above sea level, Mt. San Jacinto is the second highest peak in Southern California. Located in a remote area in the wilderness, hikers enjoy the contrast Mt. San Jacinto offers with the San Bernardino National Forest surrounding the mountain range. The Cactus-to-Clouds Trail takes you from the desert to the subalpine peak. The San Jacinto Peak Trail is 11 miles round trip with a 2,300-foot elevation gain that takes around five to six hours to complete. This trailhead is accessed via the Palm Springs Aerial Tramway, and although it is one of the lower effort trails, it's still difficult.

Best Time to Visit: The best time to visit Mt. San Jacinto is between May and October.

Pass/Permit/Fees: There is no fee to visit Mt. San Jacinto, but a $5 Wilderness Camping Permit is required.

Closest City or Town: Palm Springs, California

Physical Address:
San Bernardino National Forest
602 S. Tippecanoe Avenue
San Bernardino, CA 92408

GPS Coordinates: 33.8145° N, 116.6792° W

Did You Know? Mt. San Jacinto is one of 59 named mountains in the range.

Palm Springs

A resort city located in Riverside County, Palm Springs became a popular recreational destination in the early 1900s, when tourists with health conditions began arriving to take advantage of the area's dry heat. The Oasis Hotel, which was designed by Frank Lloyd Wright, was built in 1924, and the El Mirador followed in 1927. Additional luxury hotels cropped up in the 1930s as the area became popular with movie stars, including Charles Farrell, Ralph Bellamy, and Pearl McCallum. Today, tourism is still a major part of the city's economy, with more than 1.6 million visitors flocking to the area each year.

Best Time to Visit: The best time to visit Palm Springs is between January and April when the weather is warm and dry but not too hot.

Pass/Permit/Fees: There is no fee to visit Palm Springs.

Closest City or Town: Palm Springs, California

Physical Address:
Palm Springs Visitors Center
2901 N Palm Canyon Drive
Palm Springs, CA 92262

GPS Coordinates: 33.8926° N, 116.6093° W

Did You Know? There are more than 130 resorts and hotels and 100 restaurants in Palm Springs.

Alamere Falls

Located on Point Reyes National Seashore, Alamere Falls is a 40-foot waterfall that cascades over a cliff onto the south end of Wildcat Beach and directly into the Pacific Ocean. While it requires a 13-mile roundtrip hike to get to the falls, it is still a popular destination because of its incredible beauty. There is no park-sanctioned trail to Alamere Falls, so visitors who wish to hike to the falls are subject to an unmaintained path that could include eroding cliffs, poison oak, ticks, and other hazards. Keep in mind that there is also no cell phone service in this area. Only experienced hikers should attempt this hike.

Best Time to Visit: The best time to visit Alamere Falls is during September and October.

Pass/Permit/Fees: There is no fee to visit Alamere Falls.

Closest City or Town: Point Reyes Station, California

Physical Address:
1 Bear Valley Road
Point Reyes Station, CA 94956

GPS Coordinates: 37.9573° N, 122.7839° W

Did You Know? Alamere Falls is one of 34 waterfalls in the entire world that flows into an ocean. Only four of these are in the U.S.

Cypress Tree Tunnel

Located on the Point Reyes National Seashore, the Cypress Tree Tunnel is a spot where dozens of cypress trees have grown over the road to form a tunnel. This phenomenon is not on the park map, but the visitors center will tell you it's located halfway between there and the lighthouse. You can see the trees for at least a mile before you actually arrive at the spot. This tunnel is one of the most photographed features of the park, despite not being an official attraction. The cypress trees that make up the tunnel were planted around 1930.

Best Time to Visit: The best time to visit the Cypress Tree Tunnel is during the spring (if it's been raining, there will be fewer people there to block your photographs).

Pass/Permit/Fees: There is no fee to visit the tunnel.

Closest City or Town: Point Reyes Station, California.

Physical Address:
17400 Sir Francis Drake Boulevard
Point Reyes Station, CA 94956

GPS Coordinates: 38.0949° N, 122.9455° W

Did You Know? The Art Deco-style building at the end of the Cypress Tree Tunnel was built around the same time the trees were planted (1929-1931) and was used for ship-to-shore communications.

Point Reyes National Seashore

Point Reyes National Seashore is a park preserve located in Marin County that was established to protect the Point Reyes Peninsula from development. The seashore boasts the cleanest beaches in the state, which include wild coastal beaches, uplands, and estuaries. Parts of the park are private land used for cattle grazing, but most of the area is open to the public for hiking, wildlife observation, and visiting historical landmarks.

Best Time to Visit: The best time to visit Point Reyes National Seashore is between April and May to see blooming wildflowers.

Pass/Permit/Fees: There is no fee to visit.

Closest City or Town: Point Reyes Station, California

Physical Address:
Bear Valley Visitor Center
1 Bear Valley Visitor Center Access Road
Point Reyes Station, CA 94956

GPS Coordinates: 38.0522° N, 122.8664° W

Did You Know? Over 30,000 acres of Point Reyes National Seashore is designated as the "Phillip Burton Wilderness."

Burney Falls

Within the Cascade Range and Modoc Plateau lies a region known as McArthur-Burney Falls Memorial Park, home to the 129-foot Burney Falls. While not the largest or highest waterfall in California, it is truly magnificent. The water flows year-round, fed by both the creek above and an underground river behind the falls, which provides a lovely cascading water scene. There are five miles of trails within the park to explore, including the Burney Falls Trail Loop, which is suitable for hikers of all skill levels.

Best Time to Visit: The best time to visit Burney Falls is between spring and autumn.

Pass/Permit/Fees: There is a $10 fee per vehicle during the day. To stay overnight will be a $30 fee for one vehicle and a $10 fee for each additional overnight vehicle.

Closest City or Town: Redding, California

Physical Address:
Burney Falls State Park
24898 CA-89
Burney, CA 96013

GPS Coordinates: 41.0121° N, 121.6518° W

Did You Know? Theodore Roosevelt referred to Burney Falls as the "eighth wonder of the world."

Mount Shasta

If mountain climbing is on your bucket list, the peak of Mount Shasta should interest you as the largest volcanic peak in the contiguous United States. At an elevation of 14,000 feet, it is the fifth highest peak in California. Skilled mountain climbers may reach the peak but beware of the skill and equipment required. There are also easier paths full of wildflowers and forests for an alternate scenic route. The 14-mile drive is highly recommended, as there are seven viewpoints around the area to simply take in the sight of Mount Shasta from a distance. On a clear day, the mountain is reflected in Lake Siskiyou.

Best Time to Visit: Visit between April and September.

Pass/Permit/Fees: Each person entering the wilderness needs a free Wilderness Pass. If you plan to climb above 10,000 feet, you will also need a Summit Pass, which costs $25 per person and is valid for three days.

Closest City or Town: Redding, California

Physical Address:
Shasta National Forest Headquarters
3644 Avtech Parkway
Redding, CA 96002

GPS Coordinates: 41.4099° N, 122.1949° W

Did You Know? Mount Shasta has been the subject of an unusually large number of legends and myths.

Shasta Lake

At 30,000 acres, Shasta Lake is the largest man-made lake in California. It is a popular destination for water sports, including fishing and jet skiing. There are 370 miles of shoreline that provide other land-based activities and a 602-foot dam that is the second-largest concrete dam in the United States. The lake is located in northern California on the upper Sacramento River and generates power and irrigation to various municipalities in 29 of California's 58 counties.

Best Time to Visit: The best time to visit Shasta Lake is from mid-June to mid-September.

Pass/Permit/Fees: There is no fee to visit most of Shasta Lake, but Baily Cove requires an $8 fee.

Closest City or Town: Redding, California

Physical Address:
Redding Visitors Bureau
1321 Butte Street, Suite 100
Redding, CA 96001

GPS Coordinates: 40.8577° N, 122.2990° W

Did You Know? Woody Guthrie wrote the iconic American song, "This Land is Your Land" while helping build part of the Shasta Lake dam.

Big Bear Lake

The Big Bear Lake area is more than a lake; it's also the name of the nearby alpine town, located in a forest and mountainous environment. The San Bernardino Forest and Mountains surround the city, offering various recreational activities. The four-season mountain lake features fishing year-round and 22 miles of shoreline. Along with the 7-mile lake, Big Bear Mountain Resort has skiing and snowboarding in the winter and mountain biking in the summer. There are more than 60 miles of cross-country trails for hikers and bikers, zip-line tours, helicopter tours, and the Big Bear Jeep Experience.

Best Time to Visit: Visit during spring and winter for water and snow sports, respectively.

Pass/Permit/Fees: A permit is required for vessels (fees vary). Adventure Passes are $5 per person.

Closest City or Town: San Bernardino, California

Physical Address:
Big Bear Lake Visitor Center
40824 Big Bear Boulevard
Big Bear Lake, CA 92315

GPS Coordinates: 34.2439° N, 116.9114° W

Did You Know? Big Bear Lake was actually made using dams.

Cabrillo National Monument

Cabrillo National Monument commemorates the first time a European expedition set foot on what would later become the west coast of the United States. Juan Rodriguez Cabrillo landed at the southern tip of the Point Loma Peninsula, the future San Diego Bay, on September 28, 1542. In 1932, the landing site was designated as a California Historical Landmark, and in 1966 it was listed on the National Register of Historic Places. Each October, the annual Cabrillo Festival Open House celebrates the landing with a re-enactment of Cabrillo's expedition near the monument.

Best Time to Visit: The best time to visit is during October when the Cabrillo Festival is held.

Pass/Permit/Fees: There is a $10 fee per person.

Closest City or Town: San Diego, California

Physical Address:
1900 Cabrillo Memorial Drive
San Diego, CA 92106

GPS Coordinates: 32.6736° N, 117.2425° W

Did You Know? The Old Point Loma Lighthouse is the highest point in the park and houses the National Soaring Museum, which commemorates flight in the area.

Sunset Cliffs

Sunset Cliffs Natural Park spans 68 acres and is located in the Point Loma neighbourhood of San Diego. This patch of coastline is beautiful and serene, featuring sheer cliffs, beaches, and caves. However, be sure to watch your footing when exploring. A popular surfing spot, this area also offers panoramic views of dramatic cliffs along the Pacific Ocean. There are several areas that make for great views, including Ladera Street, Luscomb Point, and Osprey, as well as some secret beaches for the more adventurous explorers. The Sunset Cliffs Park Trail is 1.7 miles round-trip and appropriate for all skill levels. While in the area, there is also an open ceiling sea cave to venture into, but it will only be accessible during the low or negative tide.

Best Time to Visit: The best time to visit Sunset Cliffs is near sunset between April and October.

Pass/Permit/Fees: There is no fee to visit Sunset Cliffs.

Closest City or Town: San Diego, California

Physical Address:
1253 Sunset Cliffs Boulevard
San Diego, CA 92107

GPS Coordinates: 32.7252° N, 117.2531° W

Did You Know? Sunset Cliffs are near Ocean Beach Pier, the longest pleasure pier on the West Coast.

Sturtevant Falls

Located in Angeles National Forest, Sturtevant Falls is one of the most picturesque waterfalls in the area. Reaching heights of 60 feet, Sturtevant Falls showcases the beauty of the San Gabriel mountains. There is a 3.3-mile hike to the falls, starting from Chantry Flats. Hikers will follow a creek, passing resort-era cabins in Roberts Camp. While this late 19th-century era resort camp isn't completely abandoned, it's unlikely that you'll see anyone there. Once you arrive, you will have your choice of either a paved or dirt trail to the falls. The dirt trail, which ends in Roberts Camp, is about 0.4 miles longer than the paved trail.

Best Time to Visit: The best time to visit Sturtevant Falls is in the spring or summer, after heavy rain.

Pass/Permit/Fees: There is a $5 fee per vehicle to visit Angeles National Forest and Sturtevant Falls.

Closest City or Town: San Fernando, California

Physical Address:
12371 Little Tujunga Canyon Road
San Fernando, CA 91342

GPS Coordinates: 32.2139° N, 118.0196° W

Did You Know? Sturtevant Falls was named in the top 10 southern California waterfalls by "World of Waterfalls."

Alcatraz Island

Also referred to as "The Rock," Alcatraz Island is one of the most famous landmarks in California. Between August 1934 and March 1963, Alcatraz Island was the site of a federal prison where only the worst criminals were sent. Isolated from mainland California by the cold Pacific Ocean waters, Alcatraz was declared "inescapable." This description held up until three prisoners attempted to escape in 1962 and were never seen again. While it is believed all three men drowned, no one can say for sure.

Best Time to Visit: The best times to visit Alcatraz Island are between April and May or September and October.

Pass/Permit/Fees: There are three Alcatraz Island tours available, ranging from $25 per person to $92.30 per person. Check availability on the website.

Closest City or Town: San Francisco, California

Physical Address:
San Francisco Visitor Information Center
749 Howard Street
San Francisco, CA 94103

GPS Coordinates: 37.8279° N, 122.4229° W

Did You Know? Famous criminals who did time at Alcatraz include Al Capone, Robert Franklin Stroud, George "Machine Gun" Kelly, and Mickey Cohen.

California's Pacific Coast Highway

If you're ready to take one of the most iconic road trips, look no further than California's Pacific Coast Highway. It stretches over 600 miles and provides astonishing views of mountains, trees, beaches, and endless sky. There are also surfing villages, local wineries, roadside vendors, and pioneer outposts to explore on your way. It takes about 10 hours to drive the entire stretch of the Pacific Coast Highway, which connects San Francisco to Los Angeles.

Best Time to Visit: The best times to drive the Pacific Coast Highway are late spring, summer, and early fall.

Pass/Permit/Fees: There is a $10.25 fee per vehicle to drive the Pacific Coast Highway.

Closest City or Town: San Francisco, California

Physical Address:
Golden Gate Bridge Welcome Center
1750 Lincoln Boulevard
San Francisco, CA 94129

GPS Coordinates: 34.0431° N, 118.4027° W

Did You Know? Pacific Coast Highway construction began in the 1930s and was finished in 1964.

California Street Cable Car

Located in San Francisco, the California Street Cable Car is the last manually operated cable car system in the world. It is operated by the San Francisco Municipal Railway, and out of the 213 original lines built between 1873 and 1890, only three are still in operation. There are two routes that take travelers from downtown to Fisherman's Wharf and a third route that runs along California Street. Some locals still use the cable cars for their commute to work, but this unique form of public transportation is primarily used by tourists to experience San Francisco the way early residents did.

Best Time to Visit: The best time to visit the California Street Cable Car is during the summer.

Pass/Permit/Fees: There is an $8 fee per person.

Closest City or Town: San Francisco, California

Physical Address:
Cable Car Station
2439-2401 Taylor Street
San Francisco, CA 94133

GPS Coordinates: 37.8061° N, 122.4153° W

Did You Know? The wait to ride a California Cable Car can be as long as two hours (and sometimes even longer if there is an event in town).

China Beach in San Francisco

If you're looking for a small beach that locals love, China Beach features wondrous views of both the Golden Gate Bridge and Marin Headlands and offers plenty of spots for children to play. The beach is protected on both sides by rock walls, so it can be fairly crowded during the summer when the tide is high. However, this is not a good place to swim because there are no lifeguards on duty, and the current is swift. As part of the Golden Gate National Recreation Area, there are hiking trails and caves on China Beach to explore.

Best Time to Visit: The best time to visit China Beach is during the fall, when there are fewer crowds, but the weather is still warm.

Pass/Permit/Fees: There is no fee to visit this beach.

Closest City or Town: San Francisco, California

Physical Address:
Golden Gate Bridge Welcome Center
1750 Lincoln Boulevard
San Francisco, CA 94129

GPS Coordinates: 37.7888 N, 122.4913° W

Did You Know? China Beach got its name from its time as a camp for Chinese fishermen, who would come here after they finished fishing in the bay.

Golden Gate Bridge

Designated as one of the Wonders of the Modern World by the American Society of Civil Engineers, the Golden Gate Bridge is easily one of the most iconic bridges in the United States. Measuring in at 1.7 miles, this suspension bridge spans the Golden Gate, a strati that connects San Francisco Bay with the Pacific Ocean. According to Frommer's travel guide, the Golden Gate Bridge is the most photographed bridge in the world. At the time of its completion in 1937, it was the longest (4,200 feet) and tallest (746 feet) suspension bridge.

Best Time to Visit: The bridge can be visited any time of the year, but it is best viewed when there is no fog.

Pass/Permit/Fees: There is a toll to cross the Golden Gate Bridge, which ranges from $9.05 for two-axle vehicles and motorcycles to $63.35 for seven-axle or more vehicles.

Closest City or Town: San Francisco, California

Physical Address:
The Presidio Golden Gate Bridge Welcome Center
1750 Lincoln Boulevard
San Francisco, CA 94129

GPS Coordinates: 37.8207° N, 122.4783° W

Did You Know? The Golden Gate Bridge cost $17 million to build, which is the equivalent of $404 million today.

Muir Woods

Named after famed naturalist John Muir, Muir Woods is located on Mount Tamalpais and is designated as a United States National Monument. Muir Woods is also part of the Golden Gate National Recreation area and is comprised of 554 protected acres of old-growth coast redwood. Prior to the logging industry coming to California, there were approximately two million acres of old-growth redwood forests on the coast. However, by the early 20th century, only one valley called Redwood Canyon remained untouched. This area eventually became Muir Woods.

Best Time to Visit: The best time to visit Muir Woods and avoid massive crowds is between November and April.

Pass/Permit/Fees: There is a $15 fee per person.

Closest City or Town: San Francisco, California

Physical Address:
Muir Woods Visitor Center
1 Muir Woods Road
Mill Valley, CA 94941

GPS Coordinates: 37.8977 N, 122.5809° W

Did You Know? President Theodore Roosevelt declared Muir Woods a national monument in 1908.

Sausalito

This small city is a noted artistic enclave and tourist destination. It is considered a quieter, calmer alternative to the bustling streets of San Francisco, and its convenient location at the north end of the Golden Gate Bridge makes it easily accessible to visitors. Sausalito is one of the last remaining ungated marinas in the Bay Area and serves as home to a robust houseboat community totaling over 400. The area hosts many annual events for visitors to enjoy.

Best Time to Visit: The best time to visit Sausalito is between August and October for the mildest weather.

Pass/Permit/Fees: There is no fee to visit Sausalito.

Closest City or Town: San Francisco, California

Physical Address:
Sausalito Visitor Centre and Historical Society
780 Bridgeway
Sausalito CA 94965

GPS Coordinates: 37.8580 N, 122.4806° W

Did You Know? Sausalito was a major shipbuilding center during World War II. It was also the site of an important early civil rights movement milestone in 1944 when the California Supreme Court ruled that African Americans could not be excluded from employment based on their race.

The Tech Interactive

This family-friendly science and technology facility in San Jose provides visitors with immersive activities, experimental labs, and design challenge experiences. Located in one of the most technological cities in the country, The Tech Interactive has cemented itself as a world leader in creating STEAM educational resources to develop a new generation of critical thinkers. Its mission is "to inspire the innovator in everyone," as it believes that "everyone is born an innovator who can change the world for the better."

Best Time to Visit: The Tech Interactive is open daily from 10:00 a.m. to 5:00 p.m.

Pass/Permit/Fees: There is a $25 fee for adults, and a $20 fee for students, children, and seniors.

Closest City or Town: San Jose, California

Physical Address:
201 S. Market Street
San Jose, CA 95113

GPS Coordinates: 37.3324° N, 121.8902° W

Did You Know? The Tech Interactive won the National Medal for Museum and Library Service in 2015. This is the highest honor a U.S. museum can receive.

Winchester Mystery House

The Winchester Mystery House is a historic landmark and architectural marvel located in San Jose. It was once the personal home of Sarah Lockwood Pardee Winchester. She was the heiress to much of the Winchester Repeating Arms fortune. Over the years, the original eight-room farmhouse grew into the "world's most unusual and sprawling mansion," with 160 rooms, 10,000 windows, 2,000 doors, 52 skylights, 47 stairways, 13 bathrooms, and six kitchens across 24,000 square feet.

Best Time to Visit: The Winchester Mystery House is open on weekdays from 10:00 a.m. to 5:00 p.m. and on weekends from 10:00 a.m. to 7:00 p.m.

Pass/Permit/Fees: The general mansion tour costs $41.99 for adults ages 13 to 64, $34.99 for seniors ages 65 and up, and $19.99 for children between the ages of five and 12. Children ages four and under are free.

Closest City or Town: San Jose, California

Physical Address:
525 S. Winchester Boulevard
San Jose, CA 95128

GPS Coordinates: 37.3193° N, 121.9511° W

Did You Know? The price to build the house was $5 million in 1923, which would be $71 million today.

San Luis Obispo

San Luis Obispo, known locally as SLO, sits about halfway between San Francisco and Oakland in the north and Los Angeles in the south. SLO is a popular tourist destination as it is home to the central coast wine region, in addition to a vibrant downtown shopping district.. SLO is also home to California Polytechnic State University, which is also the city's largest employer. The city is known for the Madonna Inn, the Fremont Theater, Bubblegum Alley, and the Palm Theatre, which hosts the San Luis Obispo International Film Festival.

Best Time to Visit: The best time to visit San Luis Obispo is during the spring, between February and May.

Pass/Permit/Fees: There is no fee to visit San Luis Obispo.

Closest City or Town: San Luis Obispo, California

Physical Address:
San Luis Obispo Chamber of Commerce Visitor Information Center
895 Monterey Street
San Luis Obispo, CA 93401

GPS Coordinates: 35.2817° N, 120.6624° W

Did You Know? One unusual attraction in San Luis Obispo is Bubblegum Alley, where people have been sticking their chewed-up gum on walls since 1960.

Hearst Castle

Best known as the home of William Randolph Hearst, the land was purchased by his father, George Hearst, in 1865. William inherited the thousands of acres in 1919 following his mother's death, and soon after, he commissioned the design and construction of the castle. This home hosted numerous parties attended by celebrities and famous public figures within its 165 rooms and 123 acres of walkways, gardens, pools, and terraces. The castle was designed by noted architect Julia Morgan.

Best Time to Visit: The Hearst Castle is open daily from 8:00 a.m. to 6:00 p.m.

Pass/Permit/Fees: There are various tours visitors can take of the Hearst Castle, which range in price from $25 per adult and $12 per child (ages five to 12) to $100 per adult and child.

Closest City or Town: San Simeon, California

Physical Address:
750 Hearst Castle Road
San Simeon, CA 93452

GPS Coordinates: 35.6858° N, 121.1680° W

Did You Know? The Casa Grande of the Hearst Castle is 68,500 square feet and consists of 38 bedrooms, 30 fireplaces, 42 bathrooms, and 14 sitting rooms.

Cachuma Lake

Created as a result of the 201-foot Bradbury Dam in 1953, Cachuma Lake is a popular destination for kayaking, canoeing, and boating. However, swimming is not allowed, as surrounding communities depend on this lake for drinking water. As such, Cachuma Lake is not as crowded as other lakes that allow water activities, such as wakeboarding and water-skiing. This makes it an ideal location for quiet reflection. RV, tent, cabin, and yurt rentals are all available near Cachuma Lake, and boat rentals are available from the bait and tackle shop nearby. Within the park, there are also five miles of hiking trails.

Best Time to Visit: The best time to visit Cachuma Lake is during the summer.

Pass/Permit/Fees: There is a $10 fee per vehicle to visit Cachuma Lake.

Closest City or Town: Santa Barbara, California

Physical Address:
Santa Barbara Visitor Center
120 State Street
Santa Barbara, CA 93101

GPS Coordinates: 34.5841° N, 119.9498° W

Did You Know? Cachuma Lake takes its name, which means "sign," from a Chumash village.

Channel Islands National Park

Channel Islands National Park encompasses 249,561 acres. Humans have been living on the islands for at least 37,000 years, but Europeans didn't find them until 1542. The five islands that make up Channel Islands National Park are Santa Cruz, San Miguel, Santa Rosa, Anacapa, and Santa Barbara. The largest island, Santa Cruz, is the easiest one to travel to and provides the most recreational activities.

Best Time to Visit: Visit in the spring and fall seasons when the waters are less choppy and the weather is warm.

Pass/Permit/Fees: The ferry costs $97 round trip for adults between the ages of 13 and 54, $93 for children between the ages of three and 12, and free for children under the age of three and seniors aged 55 and older.

Closest City or Town: Santa Barbara, California

Physical Address:
The Robert J. Lagomarsino Visitor Center at Channel Islands National Park
1901 Spinnaker Drive
Ventura, CA 93001

GPS Coordinates: 34.1183° N, 119.7658° W

Did You Know? When visiting Channel Islands National Park in the winter, guests can view migrating gray whales.

Natural Bridges State Beach

This 65-acre state park, named for the natural bridges that formed across sections of the beach, also features tidal pools and monarch migrations. The three original arches formed over a million years ago and were once part of a large cliff that jutted out into the sea. Wave and wind erosion turned two of them into islands, and only the arch from the middle of the bridge remains. The Monarch Grove in the park has been declared a natural preserve and is home to up to 150,000 monarch butterflies from October through early February.

Best Time to Visit: The best time to visit Natural Bridges State Beach is between late October and November for monarchs. The park is open year-round.

Pass/Permit/Fees: There is a $10 fee per vehicle and a $10 parking fee.

Closest City or Town: Santa Cruz, California

Physical Address:
2531 W Cliff Drive
Santa Cruz, CA 95060

GPS Coordinates: 36.9503° N, 122.0576° W

Did You Know? The tidepools are full of colorful sea anemones, sea stars, and hermit crabs.

Santa Cruz Beach Boardwalk

As the oldest amusement park in California, Santa Cruz Beach Boardwalk is a must-visit attraction. It's also one of the last remaining seaside amusement parks on the Pacific coast and has remained a popular destination for both locals and tourists. The entire boardwalk property is designated as a California Historic Landmark, dating back to 1865 when it opened as a public bathhouse. The original was so popular that other bathhouses cropped up, and eventually, concession stands, rides, curio shops, photo stands, and more arrived to meet visitor demand

Best Time to Visit: The rides at the Santa Cruz Beach Boardwalk are open from 12:00 p.m. to 5:00 p.m. daily in the summer and on weekends in the winter.

Pass/Permit/Fees: Entrance to the Santa Cruz Beach Boardwalk is free, but each activity has its own rates.

Closest City or Town: Santa Cruz, California

Physical Address:
400 Beach Street
Santa Cruz, CA 95060

GPS Coordinates: 36.9652° N, 122.0187° W

Did You Know? The 1924 Giant Dipper wooden roller coaster and the Looff Carousel are both designated National Historic Landmarks.

The Mystery Spot

The Mystery Spot is an area of about 150 feet in diameter in which there is a gravitational anomaly. The Mystery Spot opened to the public in 1940, and since then, hundreds of thousands of visitors have been puzzled by the strange occurrences at this site. There are many theories about why gravity acts differently here, but the actual cause remains a mystery. Take a 45-minute guided tour and see if you can figure it out!

Best Time to Visit: The Mystery Spot is open Monday through Friday from 10:00 a.m. to 4:00 p.m. and Saturday and Sunday from 10:00 a.m. to 5:00 p.m.

Pass/Permit/Fees: There is an $8 fee per person for visitors ages four and up. Children ages three and under are free. Parking is $5 per vehicle.

Closest City or Town: Santa Cruz, California

Physical Address:
465 Mystery Spot Road
Santa Cruz, CA 95065

GPS Coordinates: 37.0178° N, 122.0023° W

Did You Know? While you're waiting for your tour to start, embark on the Mystery Spot hiking trail, which will give you a spectacular view through the eucalyptus trees.

Santa Monica

Santa Monica is popular for its music and art exhibits and its famous pier, which offers a wide variety of entertainment. There are also three main shopping districts: Montana Avenue, the Downtown District, and Main Street. You'll find luxury boutiques on Montana Avenue and an eclectic mix of clothing and specialty retailers on Main Street. The Downtown District is a pedestrian-only shopping area that is closed to traffic so visitors can casually stroll, shop, and enjoy street performances. Santa Monica is also home to the Majestic movie theater, the oldest theater in the city, dating back to 1912.

Best Time to Visit: The best time to visit is between September and November to avoid the hottest weather.

Pass/Permit/Fees: There is no fee to visit Santa Monica.

Closest City or Town: Santa Monica, California

Physical Address:
Santa Monica Walk-In Visitor Information Center
2427 Main Street
Santa Monica, CA 90405

GPS Coordinates: 34.0103° N, 118.4961° W

Did You Know? The Santa Monica Looff Hippodrome carousel that sits on the Santa Monica Pier was built in 1909 and is registered as a National Historic Landmark.

106

Sonoma Valley

Sonoma Valley is often referred to as the "birthplace of the California wine industry," as it is home to many of the earliest vineyards and wineries in the state. Originally the location of the sole California mission under independent Mexico, the mission was quickly secularized and used to form the center of a new town called Pueblo de Sonoma. This historic plaza is still in existence today, serving as the city's focal point. As the valley started to become widely known for its fertile ground for wine grapes, more communities sprung up around Sonoma, and it is home to numerous festivals and events.

Best Time to Visit: The best time to visit Sonoma Valley is between May and October.

Pass/Permit/Fees: There is no fee to visit.

Closest City or Town: Sonoma, California

Physical Address:
Sonoma Valley Visitors Bureau
453 1st Street E
Sonoma, CA 95476

GPS Coordinates: 38.2936° N, 122.4569° W

Did You Know? According to famed author Jack London, who lived on a ranch in Sonoma Valley, the Native American word "Sonoma" means "valley of the moon."

Emerald Bay Beach

Officially registered as a national landmark, Emerald Bay Beach is Lake Tahoe's crown jewel and one of the most photographed spots in the U.S. The depth and incredible clarity of the water offer a surreal landscape of deep turquoise blues and greens set against the mountainous backdrop. Inspiration Point is an iconic stop along Highway 89 that overlooks the vibrant landscape of the area. It also offers a view of Fannette Island, located in the middle of the bay. Trail hiking, water sports, and kayaking are some of the activities that visitors can enjoy while exploring the region.

Best Time to Visit: The best time to visit Emerald Bay Beach is during the spring.

Pass/Permit/Fees: There is a $10 entrance fee to visit Emerald State Park.

Closest City or Town: South Lake Tahoe, California

Physical Address:
138 Emerald Bay Road
South Lake Tahoe, CA 96150

GPS Coordinates: 38.9542° N, 120.1104° W

Did You Know? In 1994, Emerald Bay was also designated as an underwater state park. Artifacts lie on the seabed, all viewable via scuba diving.

Crystal Cave

Crystal Cave is a marble karst cave, polished by streams and featuring stalactites and stalagmites. The main attraction of Sequoia National Park, Crystal Cave, is only open in the summer. The road to the cave, Crystal Cave Road, is narrow and winding, so no large vehicles over 22 feet or with towing trailers are allowed. You should plan about two hours total for a visit: one hour to tour and 30 minutes each way to drive the road. Once you arrive, you'll start on the trail to the entrance of the cave, which is a half-mile of gorgeous views. The highly detailed formations in the cave are extremely fragile, so the only way to visit is on a guided tour.

Best Time to Visit: Visit Crystal Cave in the summer.

Pass/Permit/Fees: There is an $18 fee per person to visit Crystal Cave; be sure to book a tour in advance.

Closest City or Town: Three Rivers, California

Physical Address:
Sequoia National Park
47050 Generals Highway
Three Rivers, CA 93271

GPS Coordinates: 36.5874° N, 118.8304° W

Did You Know? Crystal Cave contains over three miles of passages.

General Sherman

General Sherman is located in Sequoia National Park and is the largest tree in the world. While it is not the tallest at 275 feet, its diameter is 36 feet at the base, making it the overall largest tree measured by volume. It is estimated to be 2,300 to 2,500 years old and is a giant sequoia tree. The trail leading to General Sherman is appropriately named the Sherman Tree Trail and features a walk-up platform for a closer view of the behemoth tree. There are also several other trails to explore in the surrounding area for more views of the giant sequoia trees.

Best Time to Visit: Visit General Sherman in late May or early September to avoid crowds.

Pass/Permit/Fees: There is a $35 fee per vehicle to visit General Sherman ($30 per motorcycle or $20 per individual on foot or bike. Valid for seven days)

Closest City or Town: Three Rivers, California

Physical Address:
Sequoia National Park
47050 Generals Highway
Three Rivers, CA 93271

GPS Coordinates: 36.5819° N, 118.7511° W

Did You Know? General Sherman is still growing, adding about 0.4 inches in diameter each year.

Trona Pinnacles

Located in the California Desert National Conservation Area, the Trona Pinnacles feature tufa towers, tombstones, ridges, and cones that were formed between 10,000 and 100,000 years ago. They were all formed underwater during three different ice ages and are mainly composed of calcium carbonate, or tufa. The tufas are located in the Searles Lake basin, which was once an ancient lakebed. Within the 3,800 acres are 500 tufa spires that measure as high as 140 feet.

Best Time to Visit: The best time to visit Trona Pinnacles is in the colder months around sunset.

Pass/Permit/Fees: Please refer to the Bureau of Land Management's website for current camping, permit, and fee requirements as they change depending on the season.

Closest City or Town: Trona, California

Physical Address:
Searles Valley Historical Society
13193 Main Street
Trona, CA 93562

GPS Coordinates: 35.6177° N, 117.3681° W

Did You Know? The Trona Pinnacles have been the backdrop for more than a dozen hit movies, television series, commercials, and music videos.

Lava Beds National Monument

Encompassing over 46,000 acres, Lava Beds National Monument features more than 700 caves, though approximately only 20 are accessible. Volcanic eruptions have created a diverse and rugged landscape over the years, and these caves are actually lava tubes that formed from past eruptions. Most of the developed caves are located along Cave Loop, though Mushpot Cave is the only lighted cave at Lava Beds. The caves are listed by difficulty: least, moderate, and most challenging. Along with Mushpot, Crystal Cave, Sunshine Cave, Golden Dome Cave, and Skull Cave are all popular attractions. The 13 above-ground trails feature incredible views of the lava fields, wilderness, and wildflowers when in bloom. There are also cinder cones, pit craters, and spatter cones around the area.

Best Time to Visit: There is no best time to visit the Lava Beds National Monument, as it is fantastic all year.

Pass/Permit/Fees: There is a $20 fee to visit the lava beds.

Closest City or Town: Tulelake, California

Physical Address:
1 Indian WI
Tulelake, CA 96134

GPS Coordinates: 41.7749° N, 121.5070° W

Did You Know? This area also features historical sites of the Modoc Indian War of 1872-1873.

112

Joshua Tree National Park

Joshua Tree National Park features trees, giant granite boulders, and mountains. The landscape has often been described as lunar, and people often use terms like spiritual or magical to describe how they feel about this area. The most popular things to do are hiking among the trees, rock climbing, stargazing, and taking photographs. The park is located where the Mojave and Colorado Deserts meet. The Hidden Valley area and trail are easily accessible, leading to the monolith known as the Great Burrito.

Best Time to Visit: The best times to visit Joshua Tree National Park are in the spring or fall to avoid the searing heat of Southern California.

Pass/Permit/Fees: There is a $25 fee per vehicle to visit Joshua Tree National Park.

Closest City or Town: Twentynine Palms

Physical Address:
Joshua Tree Visitor Center
6554 Park Boulevard
Joshua Tree, CA 92252

GPS Coordinates: 33.8734° N, 115.9010° W

Did You Know? The entire park is nearly 800,000 acres and is designated as an International Dark Sky Park and offers a great chance to view the stars and Milky Way.

Moaning Cavern

Named for the rock formations and sounds caused by dripping water, Moaning Cavern is a deep, vertical cave chamber. One of the few caves of this nature in the United States, Moaning Cavern offers one of the longest rappels in the country and is so tall that it could hold the Statue of Liberty. At Moaning Caverns Adventure Park, there are guided walking tours, such as the Spiral Tour, which descends 16 stories underground via a spiral staircase. The Expedition Trip takes you through the unlit areas of the cave, and the Adventure Trip features the 165-foot rappel to the bottom and takes about three hours.

Best Time to Visit: Visit during the winter.

Pass/Permit/Fees: The Spiral Tour is $20 per person, the Expedition Trip is $95 per person, and the Adventure Trip is $200-$300 per person.

Closest City or Town: Vallecito, California

Physical Address:
Moaning Caverns Adventure Park
5350 Moaning Cave Road
Vallecito, CA 95251

GPS Coordinates:38.0690° N, 120.4661° W

Did You Know? Moaning Cavern holds some of the oldest human remains discovered in the U.S.

114

Venice Beach

Founded in 1905 as a seaside resort town, Venice Beach is popular for its canals, beach, and Ocean Front Walk. Along the Ocean Front Walk, which is a 2.5-mile pedestrian promenade, visitors enjoy various street performers, vendors, and fortune-tellers. Developer Abbot Kinney established Venice, which was originally called Venice of America, to be modeled after the city in Italy. Several miles of canals were dug to drain the area's marshes so that a residential community could be built. However, these actually played into the Venetian theme, which was further enhanced by Venetian architecture and a sloping beach.

Best Time to Visit: The best time to visit is from September to November when the city is less crowded.

Pass/Permit/Fees: There is no fee to visit Venice Beach.

Closest City or Town: Venice Beach, California

Physical Address:
Venice Beach Boardwalk
1800 Ocean Front Walk
Venice, CA 90291

GPS Coordinates: 33.9984° N, 118.4809° W

Did You Know? Famous murals line the boardwalk, including *Endangered Species* by Emily Winters, *Morning Shot* by Rip Cronk, and *Touch of Venice* by Jonas.

Inspiration Point - Channel Islands

Only 14 miles off the coast of California, Channel Islands National Park is a series of five islands that are remote and feature untouched beauty. Inspiration Point is found on Anacapa Island and is the main attraction. This viewpoint offers stunning vistas of the middle island and two other parts of the Anacapa. In addition to Inspiration Point, there is a kelp forest and a beautiful lighthouse on the southern tip of the island. Visitors can kayak to explore the caves and island from the water while also checking out the multiple coves and diverse wildlife, including dolphins, whales, and seals. The Landing Cove is where the boat backs in to pick up and drop off on Anacapa.

Best Time to Visit: There is no inopportune time to visit Inspiration Point in the Channel Islands.

Pass/Permit/Fees: There is no fee to visit Inspiration Point, but there is a $60-$85 fee per day for a round-trip boat ride, and an $80 fee for a camping trip and round-trip boat ride, or a $15 fee for camping only.

Closest City or Town: Ventura, California

Physical Address:
1901 Spinnaker Drive
Ventura, CA 93001

GPS Coordinates: 34.0044° N, 119.3996° W

Did You Know? There are foxes on the Channel Islands.

Kings Canyon

The drive into Kings Canyon offers views of massive canyons, waterfalls, and a river. Down in the heart of Kings Canyon is a walking trail into Zumwalt Meadows, which is surrounded by mountainous views. The drive to reach Road's End, the end of Hwy 180, is called the Kings Canyon Scenic Byway. At 50 miles long, it starts at Hume Lake District and takes you into the valley of Kings Canyon and Cedar Grove. The loop trail near Cedar Grove takes you to the point, features wildflowers, and is an easy trek.

Best Time to Visit: The best time to visit Kings Canyon is between mid-May and mid-October

Pass/Permit/Fees: There is a $35 fee per vehicle, a $40 fee per motorcycle, or a $20 fee per individual on foot or bicycle.

Closest City or Town: Visalia, California

Physical Address:
Sequoia National Park
47050 Generals Highway
Three Rivers, CA 93271

GPS Coordinates: 36.8879° N, 118.5551° W

Did You Know? Kings Canyon is deeper than the Grand Canyon and reaches up to 8,200 feet in depth.

Cathedral Peak

Cathedral Peak is a prominent cathedral-shaped peak located in the Cathedral Mountain Range at Yosemite National Park. The peak was originally formed by glacial activity and remains uneroded because it exists above the Pleistocene glaciers. Cathedral Peak is the youngest rock formation in the Tuolumne Intrusive Suite, a group of intrusions in the Sierra Nevada Batholith that were formed 83 million years ago. In fact, one of the most popular activities in Yosemite National Park is climbing Cathedral Peak. Keep in mind that this is a moderately difficult climb and takes about an hour.

Best Time to Visit: Climbing Cathedral Peak is best between May and September.

Pass/Permit/Fees: There is a $35 fee per vehicle to visit.

Closest City or Town: Yosemite Valley, California

Physical Address:
Yosemite Valley Visitor Center
9035 Village Drive
Yosemite Valley, CA 95389

GPS Coordinates: 37.8506 N, 119.4062° W

Did You Know? Noted naturalist John Muir climbed Cathedral Peak in 1869, which inspired his book "My First Summer in the Sierra."

Glacier Point

For an outstanding view of Yosemite Valley, Yosemite
Falls, Half Dome, and Yosemite's high-country head up
7,214 feet to Glacier Point, an overlook on the south wall
of Yosemite Valley. The hike to Glacier Point is only one
mile, round trip, and will take you about 20 minutes. Once
you arrive, you'll want to hang out a while and witness one
of the most spectacular sunsets you'll ever see. In the
summer and fall, you can drive to the trail, but in the winter
and spring, the road closes due to snow, elongating the trek.

Best Time to Visit: The views are fantastic all year round,
but the road is open only in the spring and summer.

Pass/Permit/Fees: There is a $35 fee per vehicle to visit
Yosemite National Park and Mariposa Woods

Closest City or Town: Yosemite Valley, California

Physical Address:
Yosemite Valley Visitor Center
9035 Village Drive
Yosemite Valley, CA 95389

GPS Coordinates: 37.7312° N, 119.5739° W

Did You Know? Between 1917 and 1969, the Glacier
Point Hotel existed at Glacier Point. However, in the
summer of 1969 it burned down in a wildfire, along with
the McCauley's Mountain Home.

Mariposa Woods

Mariposa Woods, also known as the Mariposa Grove of Giant Sequoias, is the largest sequoia grove in Yosemite National Park. It consists of more than 500 mature giant sequoias that have been protected since President Abraham Lincoln signed legislation in 1864. This represented the first time in U.S. history that the federal government protected a scenic natural area. Ranger-led tours of Mariposa Woods are available, or if you want to venture on your own, you can hike one of the many trails.

Best Time to Visit: Mariposa Woods closes to cars between November and mid-March, so the best time to visit is between late March and October.

Pass/Permit/Fees: There is a $35 fee per vehicle to visit.

Closest City or Town: Yosemite Valley, California

Physical Address:
Yosemite Valley Visitor Center
9035 Village Drive
Yosemite Valley, CA 95389

GPS Coordinates: 37.5144° N, 119.5969° W

Did You Know? Even though Mariposa Woods is closed to vehicles in the winter, visitors can still cross-country ski and snowshoe through the trees.

Vernal Fall

This incredible 317-foot tall waterfall is located in Yosemite National Park. Unlike other major waterfalls in this park, Vernal Fall can't be seen from the road. You'll need to hike on a well-marked path beginning at the Happy Isles Nature Center. From there, the walk will be around one mile to the Vernal Fall Footbridge. or a little further to reach the top of the waterfall. Visitors often enjoy cooling off in the mist of the extremely powerful waterfall at the top. This waterfall is the result of glacier melt, so the water is extremely cold no matter what time of the year you visit.

Best Time to Visit: The best time to visit Vernal Fall is during April and May when the water is at peak flow.

Pass/Permit/Fees: There is a $35 fee per vehicle to visit Yosemite National Park and Vernal Fall.

Closest City or Town: Yosemite Valley, California

Physical Address:
Yosemite Valley Visitor Center
9035 Village Drive
Yosemite Valley, CA 95389

GPS Coordinates: 37.7286° N, 119.5439° W

Did You Know? A stamp that was issued in the Philippines in 1932 erroneously depicted Vernal Fall instead of the intended Pagsanjan Falls.

Yosemite Falls

Located in the Yosemite National Park, Yosemite Falls is one of the world's tallest waterfalls at 2,425 feet. It is actually comprised of three waterfalls: Upper Yosemite Falls, the middle cascades, and Lower Yosemite Falls. The waterfall is viewable from numerous places around Yosemite Valley. There's a one-mile loop trail that leads to the base of Lower Yosemite Falls. You can also hike to the top if you're up for a strenuous, all-day hike.

Best Time to Visit: The best time to visit Yosemite Falls is during the spring for peak water flow.

Pass/Permit/Fees: There is a $35 fee per car, $30 fee per motorcycle, or $15 fee on foot, horseback, bike, or bus to visit Yosemite Falls.

Closest City or Town: Yosemite, California

Physical Address:
Yosemite National Park
7403 Yosemite Park Way
Yosemite, CA 95389

GPS Coordinates: 37.7566° N, 119.5969° W

Did You Know? The waterfall of Yosemite Falls is fed entirely by snowmelt, so it completely dries up by August.

Proper Planning

With this guide, you are well on your way to properly planning a marvelous adventure. When you plan your travels, you should become familiar with the area, save any maps to your phone for access without internet, and bring plenty of water—especially during the summer months. Depending on which adventure you choose, you will also want to bring snacks or even a lunch. For younger children, you should do your research and find destinations that best suit your family's needs. You should also plan when and where to get gas, local lodgings, and food. We've done our best to group these destinations based on nearby towns and cities to help make planning easier.

Dangerous Wildlife

There are several dangerous animals and insects you may encounter while hiking. With a good dose of caution and awareness, you can explore safely. Here are steps you can take to keep yourself and your loved ones safe from dangerous flora and fauna while exploring:

- Keep to the established trails.
- Do not look under rocks, leaves, or sticks.
- Keep hands and feet out of small crawl spaces, bushes, covered areas, or crevices.
- Wear long sleeves and pants to keep arms and legs protected.
- Keep your distance should you encounter any dangerous wildlife or plants.

Do not rely on cell service for navigation or emergencies. Always have a map with you and let someone know where you are and how long you intend to be gone, just in case.

First Aid Information

Always travel with a first aid kit in case of emergencies.

Here are items you should be certain to include in your primary first aid kit:

- Nitrile gloves
- Blister care products
- Band-Aids in multiple sizes and waterproof type
- Ace wrap and athletic tape
- Alcohol wipes and antibiotic ointment
- Irrigation syringe
- Tweezers, nail clippers, trauma shears, safety pins
- Small zip-lock bags containing contaminated trash

It is recommended to also keep a secondary first aid kit, especially when hiking, for more serious injuries or medical emergencies. Items in this should include:

- Blood clotting sponges
- Sterile gauze pads
- Trauma pads
- Second-skin/burn treatment
- Triangular bandages/sling
- Butterfly strips
- Tincture of benzoin

- Medications (ibuprofen, acetaminophen, antihistamine, aspirin, etc.)
- Thermometer
- CPR mask
- Wilderness medicine handbook
- Antivenin

There is much more to explore, but this is a great start.

For information on all national parks, visit https://www.nps.gov/index.htm .

This site will give you information on up-to-date entrance fees and how to purchase a park pass for unlimited access to national and state parks. This site will also introduce you to all of the trails at each park.

Always check before you travel to destinations to make sure there are no closures. Some hiking trails close when there is heavy rain or snow in the area, and other parks close parts of their land for the migration of wildlife. Attractions may change their hours or temporarily shut down for various reasons. Check the websites for the most up-to-date information.